CONVERSATIONS

WITH

HISTORY

Hay House Titles of Related Interest

YOU CAN HEAL YOUR LIFE, the movie, starring Louise Hay & Friends
(available as a 1-DVD program and an expanded 2-DVD set)
Watch the trailer at: www.LouiseHayMovie.com

THE SHIFT, the movie,
starring Dr. Wayne W. Dyer
(available as a 1-DVD program and an expanded 2-DVD set)
Watch the trailer at: www.DyerMovie.com

———

ADVENTURES OF THE SOUL: Journeys Through the Physical and Spiritual Dimensions, by James van Praagh (available September 2014)

BEYOND PAST LIVES: What Parallel Realities Can Teach Us about Relationships, Healing, and Transformation, by Mira Kelley

CONVERSATIONS WITH THE OTHER SIDE, by Sylvia Browne

MIRRORS OF TIME: Using Regression for Physical, Emotional, and Spiritual Healing, by Brian L. Weiss, M.D.

THE SPIRIT WHISPERER: Chronicles of a Medium, by John Holland

All of the above are available at your local bookstore,
or may be ordered by visiting:

Hay House USA: www.hayhouse.com®
Hay House Australia: www.hayhouse.com.au
Hay House UK: www.hayhouse.co.uk
Hay House South Africa: www.hayhouse.co.za
Hay House India: www.hayhouse.co.in

CONVERSATIONS WITH HISTORY

INSPIRATION, REFLECTIONS, AND ADVICE FROM HISTORY-MAKERS AND CELEBRITIES ON THE OTHER SIDE

SUSAN LANDER

HAY HOUSE, INC.

Carlsbad, California • New York City

London • Sydney • Johannesburg

Vancouver • Hong Kong • New Delhi

Copyright © 2014 by Susan Lander

Published and distributed in the United States by: Hay House, Inc.: www.hayhouse
.com • Published and distributed in Australia by: Hay House Australia Pty. Ltd.: www
.hayhouse.com.au • Published and distributed in the United Kingdom by: Hay House
UK, Ltd.: www.hayhouse.co.uk • Published and distributed in the Republic of South
Africa by: Hay House SA (Pty), Ltd.: www.hayhouse.co.za • Distributed in Canada by:
Raincoast Books: www.raincoast.com • Published in India by: Hay House Publishers
India: www.hayhouse.co.in

Project editor: Nicolette Salamanca • Cover design: Angela Moody
Interior design: Pamela Homan

Library of Congress Cataloging-in-Publication Data

Lander, Susan, date.
  Conversations with history : inspiration, reflections, and advice from history-makers
and celebrities on the other side / Susan Lander. -- 1st edition.
    pages cm
  ISBN 978-1-4019-4537-4 (tradepaper)
  1. Celebrities--Biography--Miscellanea. 2. Biography--Miscellanea. 3. United States-
-Biography--Miscellanea. 4.   Conduct of life. 5.   Celebrities--Interviews. 6.   Spirits-
-Interviews. 7. Imaginary interviews. I. Title.
  CT105.L325 2014
  920.0973--dc23
  [B]
                                        2014008727

Tradepaper ISBN: 978-1-4019-4537-4

10 9 8 7 6 5 4 3 2 1
1st edition, August 2014

Printed in the United States of America

FSC
www.fsc.org
MIX
Paper from
responsible sources
FSC® C011935

History only comes alive
when you know the people!

CONTENTS

PREFACE

MY JOURNEY (SO FAR)

This book almost didn't get written. Four months before I started writing, I was in a coma, and the doctors didn't know if I would make it.

Like many of you reading this, I have not had an easy life. I struggled with major physical problems since I was a teenager. Despite my struggles, I earned a BA in telecommunications, then put myself through law school while working full-time. I became an attorney and worked for a labor union in Washington, D.C. Then a freak exposure to some very toxic mold pushed my already marginal health over the edge. My immune system broke down, and I became allergic to seemingly everything. Although I underwent many medical interventions,

I became sicker and sicker. These health problems cost me a career I loved, and left me with a life filled with fear, pain, and uncertainty. At one point I was living a virtually nomadic existence, moving from place to place because everything and everyone around me had the potential to make me very sick.

In 2011, I experienced a health crisis that culminated in a week-long coma. My spirit guides came to me in what I could only call a near-death experience, and asked whether I wanted to stay on Earth. They gave me three minutes to decide, saying that if I stayed, there was a big surprise in store.

They knew how to get my attention! I was very curious. What surprise could they mean? At that point, simply an end to suffering sounded pretty good. And, honestly, I felt I'd had enough surprises. But I knew in my heart that if I left, I would feel disappointed. I wouldn't have published the books that I knew I was meant to publish, and I would be leaving my family and friends. So I told my guides that I wanted to stay.

When I awoke from my coma, everything had changed. To this day, my doctors, calling my recovery "miraculous," shake their heads and say they don't understand it.

Four months later, the surprise my spirit guides promised appeared—Ben Franklin showed up in my kitchen. Thus began the parade of spirits clamoring for an interview, and when I was well enough, I wrote. I titled my book *Conversations with History,* and when it was finished, I entered it in a contest with Hay House—and won a publishing contract. No agent, no rejections, just a book contract. I am living proof that miracles can and do happen if you are walking your path.

So if you are struggling, please know that I have been there, and am still there, every day. Yet I know I am walking the path I was destined to walk here, and that makes all the difference. I can truly say that I love my life, as hard as it can be, and I am curious about what is next for me. I would like a guarantee that I will be okay (wouldn't we all?), but what I have been through has taught me to take the best possible care of myself, to participate in life, and to appreciate every minute that I'm here. (Although I have learned from my spirit friends that life on the Other Side is pretty wonderful, too.)

I look forward to sharing this journey with you because, as my celebrities in spirit remind us, we are all in this together. Life is precious. And even though it may seem otherwise, we are never alone.

The Three Questions People Always Ask

When I spoke with people during the process of writing this book, three questions came up over and over again. I would like to share them with you so you can better understand the process I went through in choosing and communicating with the spirit participants. I also briefly address the subject of life on the Other Side, as this comes up periodically in this book.

1. How Did You Choose the Participants in This Book?

The answer is: I didn't—they chose *me!* Most of it seemed orchestrated from the Other Side. Throughout the process of writing this book, I was always on the lookout for messages and signs about who should be included. Names popped into my head out of nowhere, and my attention would be drawn to songs on the radio, dialogue on TV, images in the subway, or books in the store. Spirits can be very ingenious in the ways they catch our attention, and New York City, where I live, has so much celebrity signage that it gave them lots of opportunities.

During this process I was very much the detective, looking for clues about whom to add next to my list of participants. These "hits" would be accompanied by strong feelings that this was in fact someone who wanted to be included in the book. I kept these lists up on my refrigerator and added the names of new participants as they came into my consciousness. It was a tremendously fun and magical process, and somehow I always knew the next few participants who were coming up at any given time.

Occasionally there was someone whom I personally wanted to interview. In these cases I would send out a telepathic message that I would like to talk to the poet Sappho, for example, and the New Orleans voodoo priestess Marie Laveau—and I usually got my way. But not always. For example, I wanted to interview Frida Kahlo, but when I started thinking of her, she appeared, glared at me, and asked me to please not bother her and just leave her to her painting and to her job in an art museum on the Other Side! Other times I would send out a name and hear the word *no* or just get a feeling of "dead air"—nothing was there. It was as if I were making a phone call: spirits can choose whether they want to answer. But there was no shortage of people who were eager to participate.

There were a few whom I didn't see coming, who just showed up and refused to leave. Eva Perón was one of these. She appeared one day and seemed to knock everyone else out of the way like a bowling ball sending all the pins flying. Her presence was so big and intense that I gave in and did the interview that day.

It was definitely a collaborative process. I was constantly reviewing these lists and putting the names in order. When it was a particular person's turn, I would send out a telepathic message that he or she was next, specifying good times to talk. I usually had a few questions prepared, but, as I said, some people showed up unexpectedly and I'd have to improvise.

Some of these interviews were completed in one session, but others took place over the course of weeks, months, or even a year, with participants disappearing then abruptly resurfacing with additional material. Sometimes they would just pop in and say one thing, leaving me scrambling for something to write with, and then they would disappear again. Sometimes they'd pick up where they left off on a topic from a previous session, but other times they'd go off on whole new tangents. Given the energetic challenges of mediumship, it was actually easier for me when spirits would come and go like that, breaking up the interview into a few short sessions rather than staying for one long one. Communicating across the realms takes a lot of energy, so we'd both start to wear out after a while; it would become harder and harder to hold the connection.

You'll notice that the interviews vary in length. This was due to the whims of the participants. Some of them had particular subjects that they wanted to discuss. Others just wanted to chat about Earth life again, even if only for a short time. And some just wanted to say good-bye to loved ones who were still here. Although I usually had some questions ready, the conversations were really about these souls and the messages they wanted to share—not my agenda. And when the participants were done, they were done. They would tell me when they were getting ready to leave, and I could feel their energy pulling away.

I learned to be very flexible with the process. I often had two or three unfinished interviews open at any given time, but somehow it worked. There was definitely a lot of spirit activity around me during the time I wrote this book. However, they were all very polite in their approaches, and much of our time together was planned. If they appeared and it wasn't a good time, I would just say, "Not now," and they always honored my request immediately.

My interactions with these spirits, although unusual, were much like any other type of human relationship. Sometimes we just had a nice chat, and other times we really connected and became friends. Even though this book is finished, some of these spirits—in particular Andy Warhol, Ben Franklin, Gandhi, and Sappho—still pop in and say hello! It's always nice to see them again and catch up a little.

2. How Do You Actually Communicate with These Spirits?

Although the spirits and I live in different dimensions, we were able to communicate in several ways that didn't involve speaking. Spirits don't have a body or a voice box, but they do have the ability to transmit information. They were able to connect with me primarily through my psychic senses of hearing, seeing, and feeling, and many of them were very good at it.

While I was interviewing them, I would ask questions telepathically, then wait for a response. Sometimes the answers would come in the form of words, phrases, music, or even crystal clear images that would suddenly pop into my brain. The spirits' answers often included the transmission of feelings, so I could actually experience how someone or something affected them. For example, I might suddenly be basking in a pool of love—that can feel very nice! On the other hand, a spirit would sometimes want to communicate pain and grief. That wouldn't feel so good, but that comes with the territory. When it seemed that the interviews were really finished, I would then take all of this information and put it together in a way that made sense, editing for length and clarity.

People who communicate with spirits like this are called "message mediums," and we are used to this process. With time and practice it can come very naturally. Although it can seem very mysterious, it actually works really well, and the results can be as precise as what you see in this book.

If you are interested in the science behind this type of communication, it happens through an energetic connection between spirits and the people who are able to connect with them. Although it seems to defy explanation, it's really just basic physics. Everything is made up of energy, but everything vibrates at different speeds. Spirits have a faster vibration than do our dense human bodies. However, people like me have the ability to raise our vibrations to be closer to that of spirits. Spirits lower their energy, we raise ours by getting into a meditative state, and then we are able to mesh our energies in a way that allows communication. The best way I can describe it is that our boundaries just get kind of blurry.

There are trance mediums who allow spirits to more fully inhabit their bodies and speak through them, but I am not one of them! Message mediumship works just fine for me. It's a very comfortable and respectful process. Really, it's just communication—but done on a telepathic, psychic level instead of the way humans normally communicate.

3. What Is Life Like on the Other Side?

Throughout these interviews, I would occasionally ask spirits what they're doing on the Other Side. The answer is . . . pretty much anything they want. They experience all kinds of relationships. Some have a special soul mate, which may be a romantic connection. They engage in many of the same things that we do for fun on Earth, such as spending time with friends and loved ones, and going to plays, concerts, and other cultural events. They can have a job if they so choose, and manifest homes in whatever type of environment they like. They will often study and learn new skills to better themselves and to continue to be of service. Some of this information is then imparted to people living on Earth, which results in advances in many fields such as medicine and technology.

Spirits are not limited by the constraints of time, space, a physical body, or money. They can look any way they want, any age they want, and any gender they want. They don't have to worry about gaining weight. They can eat—or not. They don't get sick, and there are healing centers on the Other Side to repair the energy of those who were ill before they passed. When spirits feel the time is right, they may incarnate again on Earth or some other place, often choosing to do so with the same group of souls. These groups of souls play different roles in each others' paths throughout different lifetimes. I believe that when we meet someone and feel as if we've known him or her forever, the person is usually part of our "soul group."

It's very hard to wrap our human brains around these concepts, but suffice it to say that spirits live a very wonderful life. The Other Side is their true Home. Earth is just a place they come to visit. There are many excellent books written about this subject. I particularly enjoy ones by scientists and doctors, such as Brian Weiss, M.D., who writes about past lives and reincarnation; and Dr. Michael Newton, who has done extensive research through hypnotherapy on the experience of "life between lives." Lisa Williams, John Holland, John Edward, and James Van Praagh are also wonderful mediums who have written insightful books on these subjects.

Finally, I will always have a special place in my heart for Sylvia Browne's *Life on the Other Side: A Psychic's Tour of the Afterlife*. It was the first book I read on the subject. Sadly, Sylvia passed on November 20, 2013. I'm sure she's just getting back into the swing of things on the Other Side and having a fabulous time. Mediums such as myself owe her a great debt of gratitude for bringing mediumship and spirit communication out into the mainstream.

INTRODUCTION

BEN FRANKLIN IN MY KITCHEN

What would you do if Ben Franklin was standing in your kitchen?

That's how this book got started. Well, actually it started with Ben Franklin's schedule.

It was the morning of September 12, 2011. I was writing another book and decided that I needed some help with discipline. Someone had sent me a copy of Franklin's schedule, his daily routine recorded in his autobiography, so I hung it up on my refrigerator, hoping that it would motivate me. It was simple and direct and right down to business—lots of time for work, "diversion" or conversation, and addressing "Powerful Goodness." Then I saw a flash of shoulder-length gray hair, gold wire-rimmed spectacles, a furrowed brow, thin-lipped smile . . . it was *him,* decked out in full colonial garb.

As I said in the Preface, I am what is called a medium—I can communicate with spirits. I can see them, hear them, and feel them. Granted, I don't usually see the spirits of famous dead people. Usually I see people's deceased loved ones or "spirit guides" (the spirits that help us walk our paths while we are here on Earth). But I was looking at Ben Franklin's schedule, so why *wouldn't* he come visit? I chalked it up to an interesting, but singular, occurrence and went on with my day.

The next day I was looking at the schedule and there he was again. Oops. Which brings me back to my original question: "What would you do if Ben Franklin was standing in your kitchen?" I decided to talk with him.

So we started talking. Although I was feeling more than a little silly, I started showing him things that an 18th-century visitor might find interesting in a modern Manhattan apartment: my computer, my sound dock with my iPhone, the microwave, the view from my 17th-floor apartment. He reacted to everything with curiosity and amazement, and I was just as curious and amazed to be talking to him.

Ben was fascinating to talk with and a very distinguished gentleman (although he says he prefers to be called a "statesman"). He was good-natured, focused, intense, and so smart, with an underlying sense of humor and sense of purpose. Though the expression on his face was often a thin smile, I also got the impression that he was about to crack a joke at any second. He told me that he loves puns and will sometimes sit and make them up, saving them to drop at an appropriate time as if he'd spontaneously come up with them right then. He said it makes him look clever—"Little do they know!"

He told me that he enjoys creating and inventing and "being of service," but feels there is "a danger in taking oneself too seriously" or "being too pious—just know who you are and go on from there." When he said this, it occurred to me that I was being given some very interesting information, and I wanted to remember everything.

So I grabbed some paper, dated it, and started writing. Then I began asking him questions. (Twenty years in the legal field has taught me how to ask a good interview question.)

And that is how *Conversations with History* was born. As a matter of fact, Ben gave this book its name. Since then, the spirits haven't stopped coming, and they haven't stopped talking. The wisdom that their messages hold for all of us never ceases to amaze me.

At the beginning I kept asking myself "Why me?" and "How could this be real?" But I have come to realize that it doesn't matter. Whether or not you believe that it is real (and sometimes I do and sometimes I don't), I think that there is something fascinating and wonderful to be found in every interview. Each one is very different, although there do seem to be common threads or themes woven throughout them. I think you will find these more easily if you read the interviews in order.

What I can say is that these participants know many things I don't, and the information that came through in my interviews has taught me a great deal. What I have learned has made my life better and happier every day, and I am looking forward to sharing it all with you. There are lessons in abundance and prosperity, love and relationships, personal responsibility for the world around us, and the legacy we will leave for future generations.

The historical figures who "knocked" and came forward to participate are a very interesting and eclectic group. Most of the participants seemed to have chosen me. I had barely even heard of some of them. But I chose a few others whom I was personally interested in, asked if they would participate, and was happy I got to talk with them.

There were those with whom I really didn't want to talk, but I felt that I needed to (for example, Leni Riefenstahl, who was infamous for making films about Hitler in World War II that were felt to be Nazi propaganda). Most of these folks have vastly different areas of knowledge and expertise from me. I have some experience in social justice and politics from my 20 years in the legal field, but that's about it. I spent my career writing legal briefs and technical pieces.

Included in these interviews are actors, abolitionists, extremely successful businessmen, artists, spiritual leaders, a king, a warrior, a poet, musicians, a prophet, and a voodoo priestess. One of the participants passed away sometime in the 6th century B.C., while the most recent passed in 2011. In his interview, Einstein talks about the nature of time and how to make it work for you; I think I got a C-minus in physics. The ancient Greek poet Sappho gave me some new poems; I can't write a poem to save my life . . . You get the picture. So much in these interviews is outside the realm of my experience. To me that is what made it so illuminating, personally challenging, and *fun* to work on.

By the way, I have always been a terrible history student. But after writing this book, I am proud to say that I'm not quite as bad as I used to be.

How This Book Is Set Up

The book is broken up into 22 chapters, one for each spirit's interview. At the beginning of the chapter is some basic biographical information as well as my initial impressions of the participant. I included each person's cause of death, often in their own words, because some turned out to be particularly interesting. For example, Ben Franklin described his cause of death as "Old age. Past my body's expiration date." It sounds like Ben!

I conclude each chapter with my final thoughts after the interview and sometimes recommend further reading (for example, autobiographies) for those who would like to learn more about these fascinating people.

In case you were wondering, I didn't research these pieces beforehand. I occasionally did a few minutes of Internet research—sometimes while the spirits were visiting—if I felt I didn't know enough about the current interview subject. A perfect example was Abbie Hoffman. My initial thought about him was, *Wasn't he the guy who wore the stars-and-stripes shirt?* (Sorry, Abbie.) My intention was to learn just enough so I could ask a few intelligent questions, while taking care not to learn so much that I became biased.

After the interviews, I looked up some of the specific information that I received, and when I found a source that validated or further explained it, I included it. Later, in writing this book, I did a little more research in order to construct the biographies.

———

My hope is that you will read and enjoy these interviews, and that they will give you something new to think about. This is a wonderful, interesting bunch of folks. Through this project I came to love (or at least respect) them all. Their hearts and their humanity shine through, and I think that they have much down-to-earth wisdom to share with us.

———

CHAPTER 1

BEN FRANKLIN

Benjamin Franklin was a founding father of the United States. He was an author, printer, scientist, inventor, politician, postmaster, diplomat, activist, satirist, and musician. He was well known for his life-changing inventions (including bifocals and the Franklin wood-burning stove) as well as his discoveries and theories regarding electricity.

He was born on January 17, 1706, in Boston, Massachusetts, and lived much of his life in Philadelphia, Pennsylvania. He died on April 17, 1790, at the age of 84.

It was completely shocking to have him show up in my kitchen more than 220 years later.

The Interview

[I'm writing and trying to think of questions to ask him.]

Ben Franklin: I am glad you write; it's "the lost art of the pen."

Susan Lander: What are you doing these days?

BF: Working on circuits on the Other Side—computers—to make them lightning fast and even smaller. Eye-activated like Stephen Hawking uses, but available to everyone as a matter of course. The computer follows the energy and focus of the eye and that activates it. You can type and search, and never need your hands or arms. Good for the infirm but just generally useful.

SL: Ben, your name has been popping up a lot this week. Did you make a decision that you wanted to be heard now for some reason?

BF: Funny you should ask. Why, yes, I feel I have something renegade and unique to offer: fiscal responsibility, heart, science, and discipline. All important, but becoming lost arts. It doesn't need to be directly attributable to me, although I would appreciate it if it was. I think the modern-day world is fascinating—not only for its possibilities, but for its doom-and-gloom attitude. It is truly a world of paradox that you live in now.

Look at all you have! Hard things, easy things, modern conveniences—technology especially. And yet most people living on Earth today barely give it a thought. Yet there exists so much pain and poverty, some of it a direct consequence of the modern lifestyle: corporate greed; environmental destruction, such as deforestation of the jungles and rain forests; and just a general cavalier attitude.

Do people care? Yes, I believe they do. Yet they feel powerless. Given the possibilities that technology has given us in worldwide communication, we the people have never had more power individually. Yet we refuse to exercise it, believing we are powerless. We are not. We have merely to pick up the reins and follow through. And that is so often the missing ingredient. Discipline, my dear, and creativity . . . with a little luck thrown in. And knowing who your friends are and who your enemies are.

So choose carefully whatever you choose to do, and then move forward, head held up and proudly. For we are all Divine, and whatever mission we choose is part of that Divine mission. And that in and of itself makes it holy regardless of the outcome; and you are holy, and what you do is holy and in service of all mankind. Never forget that. It is the same whether it be on a grand scale or mundane. Do you understand?

[I am drinking jasmine tea. Ben notices.]

BF: Aah, that smell of jasmine. I do miss my physical senses. But the physical body can come with much hardship as well. Do not forget to enjoy your senses while you're here.

SL: Thank you, Ben!

BF: *[laughs]* My pleasure, my dear. Thank you for listening and being willing to write with an open mind and an open spirit.

SL: It just occurred to me that your spirit name isn't "Ben Franklin"!

BF: Of course not. But as you know, our names are irrelevant. Our countenances are irrelevant. Our souls are stable and immutable, yet evolving, and eternally beautiful. We are who we are, and that never changes. And thank God for that—I do like a little certainty, stability, and continuity. Gets me through the day gracefully.

I love that you have my schedule posted up on your modern-day refrigerator. It makes me chuckle. I'm glad it's of use to somebody other than me!

It's beautiful where you live. Look at that view from your window; it's like soaring with the birds. Truly beautiful.

SL: Was our meeting today just a coincidence?

BF: Meet? I already know you. Why do you think you were always so interested in me? Why is my schedule on your refrigerator?

[He shows me a vision of a white horse pulling a carriage, with the horse rearing up and whinnying. It is in the 1700s in Philadelphia. This

suggests to me that Ben and I had a past-life connection in that time period.]

BF: Our connection was a possibility so that I could deliver my message to the modern-day world. My message really is very simple: always believe in yourself, love yourself, love life, do what you came here to do, and then go Home.

Many blessings to you. I must go now. Call whenever you need me—I am here, and I will arrange for it. Blessings and Godspeed. Signing off.

[Six months and many spirit interviews later, I check in with Ben.]

SL: Well, Ben, what do you think of our project now?

BF: Astounding! I am delighted with our progress. It is coming in exactly as planned, but better than I hoped. More surprises to come! Stay tuned for the coming attractions!

SL: Thank you, Ben, and Godspeed!

Reflections

Although I was very surprised to be talking with Ben, I was not surprised to learn that he is still an inventor and an innovator. It's wonderful that he's continuing to work on inventions on the Other Side that will help to improve the lives of people on Earth, particularly those who have disabilities. I think he exemplifies something that I've learned during my work with spirits: on the Other Side, we tend to be the best version of ourselves.

It was especially fun for me as a native Philadelphian to imagine that I had a past-life connection with Ben. I have always been fascinated by Colonial Philadelphia. It isn't unusual for souls to reincarnate in the same place or similar time period more than once, and past-life connections to places or time periods often cause people to feel strong, otherwise unexplained bonds.

If you would like to learn more about Ben Franklin's lifetime on Earth, he wrote *The Autobiography of Benjamin Franklin,* published in 1791.

And now we'll take a leap into the modern day, with a visit from another famous revolutionary, antiwar activist Abbie Hoffman.

CHAPTER 2

ABBIE HOFFMAN

When Abbie Hoffman first appeared to me, he was wrapped in an American flag. He was thin, with big hair and soft brown curls. He was kind of serious but had a sense of humor and an easy smile. He struck me as someone who really cared about his ideals and was willing to "walk his talk."

However, the only thing I knew about him was that he was famous for wearing a shirt decorated with the American flag. I wanted to learn more about him and that incident, so I did a little Internet research before we started the interview. I learned that he was arrested, went to trial, and was found guilty of the charge of "desecration" for wearing the American-flag shirt.

He was born Abbott Hoffman on November 30, 1936, in Worcester, Massachusetts. He was a political, civil rights, and antiwar activist (particularly taking a stand against the Vietnam War). He was also a psychologist and a writer, notably of *Woodstock Nation* (1969) and *Steal This Book* (1971). He co-founded the Youth International Party (the Yippies), a countercultural group of revolutionaries whose tenets were antiwar and pro–freedom of speech. However, their methods included street theater and political pranks, and unfortunately that kept them from being taken very seriously by the mainstream. For example, they once nominated a pig named Pigasus as a candidate for President of the United States.

But even though Abbie Hoffman enjoyed planning political pranks and grandstanding, he was no cartoon character. It seemed to me that on some level he felt misunderstood. He was steadfast in his beliefs and in his vision for a better world, and it became very clear during his interview that he remains so on the Other Side. He died on April 12, 1989, in New Hope, Pennsylvania, at the age of 52. He told me that his cause of death was "too many pills." (His death was ruled a suicide using barbiturates.) But that was just his Earth story, and that's over now.

The Interview

[Abbie begins the interview by showing me an image of a peace sign, and then sending me a string of phrases popular in the 1960s.]

Abbie Hoffman: Greetings!

Susan Lander: Greetings!

AH: Groovy, far-out, can you dig it?

SL: Are you working with Ben Franklin on this project?

AH: Of course. We're one big, chummy club up here. Thank you for taking the time to talk with us and share our messages.

We luminaries have something important to share. *[laughs]* At least we think we do! Or maybe we're just self-important, and we miss being on Earth. Either way, here we are, and thank you for listening.

SL: I keep seeing the flag image, the famous one associated with you. Can you explain why you wore it?

AH: It was the juxtaposition, the irony, of what the flag was supposed to stand for and what it did stand for. And so it is again. We are a great nation, *can* be, anyway—can you dig it? We don't have to be a nation of warmongering warlords and blank sheeplike followers kowtowing to the corporate entity.

SL: Wow! So you wore the flag, and you're still wearing it.

AH: Yes, to remind people, the masses, of what the flag could stand for. The stars and stripes being bright and not dead, trampled by morally bereft authority.

SL: Are you still angry?

AH: Yes. Power should be in the hands of the people.

SL: Can I ask you some questions?

AH: Shoot, or don't. *[smiles]*

SL: What do you think of the world today?

AH: Fucked up. Even more today than when I was here, because the political right is so much better at what it does. The masses are much more tired than they used to be. There's only so much fight left in most of us. There are a few tireless warriors like you and me, but the rest of us are just trying to get through the day.

The environment is more polluted. The distribution of wealth is more unequal. Dangerous times for you on Earth. Truly pivotal, though—there's still time to turn things around.

SL: So what would you do if you were here right now?

AH: What I do best! Talk a lot. Stir the masses. Stir the pot. Rabble-rouse. Organize labor. Organize the people. Maybe try some new strategies.

SL: Like what?

AH: Hadn't really thought about it. But I would get really good at using computers, the Internet, and the media. I think that's the key. I would give people an actual vision of how their life could be different by *showing* them. I would make promos, docudramas. Show them, empower them, and give them a tool kit. You know, *A, B, C.* Outline the next steps. Show them what they can do if they like what they see in the new vision, and don't like what they see in their everyday lives and in their bank accounts.

Money is funny, by the way. Up here it all seems so silly. Just paper, nothing. You can make it multiply. Just like turning on a faucet—I want it, turn on, here it is, boom.

SL: "Turn on." Haha.

[He's making a reference to the 1960s counterculture slogan by Timothy Leary, which was related to psychedelic drugs: "Turn on, tune in, drop out."]

AH: Thank you. I thought I fit it in pretty well myself.

SL: Did you know that marijuana still isn't legal, although it looks like we're moving toward decriminalization?

AH: I know. Unbelievable that the fight is still going on after all these years.

SL: Do you have a word for those who are still working to make it legal?

AH: Tell them to keep fighting the good fight for liberty. They will win. Tell them not to get tired, the end is near, and all of this hard work will pay off. Smoke away and enjoy it! You have that right. Thank you for fighting to give that to others.

SL: Do you have any regrets, anything you would have done differently?

AH: Yes. I would have fucked more. *[laughs]* I mean that. Smoked more . . . drugged more . . . No regrets.

SL: Would you have liked to live longer?

AH: Yes, but my body didn't want to, so I left. I was bummed out, and so was it. Too much, too soon, too fast.

SL: Are you working on any projects now? What does your typical day look like?

[In response, he is showing me an image of his life on the Other Side. He's sitting on the grass in a lush green garden. He's leaning against a white stone bench and reading a book with a red cover.]

AH: I read, think, just take it easy. But I am also involved in a group, like a think tank, that plots strategy for world peace. We meet fairly regularly, and—this is really cool—we infuse ideas into the people on Earth to speed up the process. It's working.

SL: How so?

AH: People are rising up to the cause globally. Many do believe there is a way other than war. We are putting the energy into the collective consciousness from the Other Side, and people "catch" the ideas. So now you're seeing more and more people gathering together on this peace cause. This is a very good thing. I am hopeful that we can still turn it around. I think people are tired of all the fighting, so many years of destruction and war. In our hearts, I think we all know there is a better way.

Those who are behind these wars of corporate tyranny, greed, and destruction are really just bullies. They are weak, afraid, and will cave if pushed. They are deeply afraid that their world will not stay the way it is for them. Their greatest fear is that the masses will take back their power. Deep down they know they are so outnumbered that they don't have a chance. All people have to do is stand up. I still don't understand why they won't. People don't understand their own power to move mountains.

SL: Ben Franklin also talked about reclaiming our personal power. Am I starting to see a pattern?

AH: Yes. It's more than an antiwar and antipoverty strategy; it's a fundamental spiritual truth. Understanding this will change the world as well as people's lives individually.

SL: Are you planning to come back for another lifetime? And if so, what would you work on here?

AH: I wouldn't discount it! We'll see. I'll wait and see whether the world needs me again. I would do something environmental. Maybe I'll own an organic farm. Live out in the Colorado Rockies with the goats. Be a gentleman farmer. Now wouldn't that be something!

But I know me, I wouldn't be able to keep my mouth shut and would still commute to Washington on the red-eye and plan some protests. We are who we are, after all. It doesn't matter if we're here in our spirit Home, or living on Earth. If I go back to Earth, I might like a little more balance next time, so I don't burn out so quickly. I could have a family—a wife and grandkids—and read to them. Give them good ideas for the next generation. Sounds kinda restful. I can dig it.

[He shows me an image of this future life that he is imagining. He is sitting on a porch swing with a woman in a yellow dress. They are both older. He is reading to his young grandson from a book with stars and stripes on its cover, and the cover bears his name. The whole vision feels very peaceful.]

SL: So you would come back to Earth to continue your peace work?

AH: Yes. I have a vision. I am a great patriot. I believe that we as a country and as a people can be so much better than we are. We can do so much better than we do. Until then, I'll hold that vision. People, stand up for yourselves! I understand why so many of you don't—you're tired and just trying to get through the day—but know that it can get so much better for you. Hold that vision and fight!

SL: Anything else before we end this interview, at least for now?

AH: *[smiles]* Yes. Thank you for listening and taking these messages. I enjoyed this. And to everyone, keep up the good fight. We all need to do our part, and this is yours now. Go to it.

SL: Thank you, too. What do you most want to be remembered for?

AH: For never giving up. Ever.
Thank you, signing off.

[He ends the interview the way he began it, by raising his hand, two fingers forming a peace sign.]

Reflections

I enjoyed meeting Abbie Hoffman and learning more about him. Of course he was wearing his famous shirt throughout the whole interview. He felt so alive, vibrant, and active, and I found him really inspiring. It is a testament to how important his vision is to him that he continues to work toward it while he is on the Other Side. I could feel that he really enjoyed his time on Earth, but that he had a very intense lifetime. Now that he is on the Other Side, all he wants is some peace. Peace is still what motivates him.

While he was on Earth, he felt driven to make things better, and it wasn't always easy for him. Drugs gave him a temporary break, but in the end they proved to be his undoing. Fortunately for all of us, his message, his memory, and his work toward world peace live on . . . as does his iconic American-flag shirt.

My next visitor continues exploring the theme of freedom— Frederick Douglass, who was born a slave.

CHAPTER 3

FREDERICK DOUGLASS

I felt like I was having tea with Mr. Douglass during this interview. He is a very distinguished gentleman! It seemed that we were just hanging out together and having a casual chat. I kept seeing an image of us seated at a mosaic-covered café table. He had brown skin, his face was shiny, and he had small birthmarks or moles on his face. His wiry, gray-black hair was in a side part. He was dressed according to the style of the time period in which he lived, wearing a white shirt, brown suit with thin white pinstripes, and white or cream hose.

He was a nice man, very quiet and unassuming, and easy to converse with. He had a lighter energy to him—it felt almost female at times. He was serious but not intense. When he began talking, he had a softer voice than I would have expected, and he was low-key and gentle.

Frederick Douglass was born a slave around February 1818 in Tuckahoe, Maryland (his exact date of birth is unknown). He escaped from slavery and changed his name from Frederick Augustus Washington Bailey to Frederick Douglass in order to elude slave hunters. He went on to become a leader of the abolitionist movement and, after writing his autobiography and going on a two-year speaking tour of Great Britain and Ireland, was able to officially purchase his freedom. He was a brilliant speaker and writer, particularly on abolitionist matters, as well as an editor and diplomat. He was a consultant to President Abraham Lincoln during the Civil War, and the first black citizen to hold a high rank in the U.S. government. He died on February 20, 1895, in Washington, D.C., at about the age of 77. When I asked him his cause of death, his response was, "My heart ceased to beat. It doesn't matter."

The Interview

Susan Lander: Okay, Mr. Douglass, this is your time. I am here to listen to your words, thoughts, and feelings.

Frederick Douglass: Thank you, Susan.

[I sense him waiting politely, so I begin asking him questions.]

SL: What do you think of the world today?

FD: It is not much different than when I was there. However, people do seem to be more polite, though they still have their own agendas and will push to achieve them.

You will always see the creations of the most powerful move to center stage and be in the limelight, for good or ill. This is how we create our world.

SL: What do you mean?

FD: He who moves to center stage will attract more allies, who will in turn help him to stay there. This is why the attention of the media is so very important. An astute observer will know this, see this, and use this to his advantage. It can be for good or ill, depending on who is the observer. It is all relative, you see. Judgment is in the eye of the beholder.

SL: Is there something in particular that you would like to talk about during this interview?

FD: I would like to talk about modern-day slavery.

SL: Can you be more specific?

FD: Of the masses. Again, judgment is in the eye of the beholder, so step back and get the big picture. There are in fact many evils today: poverty, crime, incest, power plays, and institutionalized violence.

SL: Can you explain what you mean by "institutionalized violence"?

FD: Violence that is sanctioned by society. *Right* and *wrong* are funny words. Their meanings are often elusive. But when we as human beings or souls look at a particular situation and say, "That's wrong," and feel it—or at least the majority of us feel that way—we have crossed that line. As so it was with slavery in ancient times, more recent times, and modern times. One example of modern-day slavery is the existence of sweatshops.

During my time on Earth, it was societally accepted that a certain group of people could be exploited physically for labor, or even sex, and be treated as less than human. This was the antithesis of the spiritual perspective. It was also a financial exploitation, you see, for the value of goods and services. This can still be seen in the exploitation of workers and of the masses that are exploited for what they can provide the wealthy. People look the other way; they feel powerless to change it.

Nowadays it is not deemed acceptable for bosses or overseers to physically beat their workers, because as a society we have made a decision that it's wrong and "we don't do that." But there seems to be a belief that as long as people aren't being beaten, all is well and we are good as people. But exploitation is exploitation, and people continue to place in power those whose decisions have that very effect—financial and personal exploitation.

There has been a societal decision that says: It is *okay* to overwork individuals. It is *okay* to pay them less than they are worth. It is *okay* to cut their wages, or increase their hours, or cut their benefits that they cherish and count on for seeing them through old age. It is *okay* that people do not have access to health care if they should become ill or infirm.

It is *not* okay, and I ask you: How is this any different than slavery? Though their employers may not beat people physically, they certainly do financially and emotionally, and their resources are exploited for the use and pleasure of the most powerful.

In other countries, people—including children—are still bought and sold like cattle and forced to work in appalling conditions. We look the other way because we don't know what to do. We don't know how to fix it, and we feel powerless to change it. Fallacy. We aren't powerless! And in this country we say, "That could never happen here. That was then, this is now." Nonsense! It is happening now, and it is happening here. Turning and looking the other way does not change it; it is still so. People, get your heads out of the sand and take responsibility. Do something to change it!

That is it—I have said my piece. Just don't fool yourselves into believing slavery is a thing of the past. It is just underground, like prohibition. People are creative and will find ways to meet their needs. And in this society, where commerce runs everything, it will always be about getting more. The better you are at it, the more you will have. The more you have, the more you will get, period. And you will find a way to keep it. For it is as if your very lives depend on it.

It is, of course, a fallacy that you must exploit others like cattle to get what you need. It is ugly, cruel, unfair, and unconscionable, and it needs to be stopped. But we can't do it from up here. Only you can, down there. So I ask: What are you going to do about it? From my perspective, we all have a moral responsibility to step in when we see cruelty and exploitation.

SL: What about judgment being "in the eye of the beholder"?

FD: Yes, but some things rise to the level of spiritual truths and spiritual necessity. Souls have the right to a certain level of treatment out of respect for their Divine natures, at least. And protecting those who can't protect themselves is important and Divine.

What is the purpose of life, after all? To collect or amass wealth, and then die? I don't believe that. Getting into that cycle is very dangerous spiritually. Like the mythical King Midas, we risk having gold all around us but nothing spiritually important to show for it. We have choices about how we live, what we stand for, and what we teach others by example. These are our own choices because we are autonomous as people and as eternal souls.

Spiritually immoral acts are not looked upon favorably over here, so you will have to answer for them, repent, and repay. There is no hell except for what we create, but karma is still a powerful thing. When you come over here, it is much easier to see the error of your ways. Ignore these basic spiritual truths and it will come back to haunt you one way or another. At the very least you will get to see, feel, and experience the pain you caused others, and that is very powerful. To some degree you must make personal amends. But still, you get to live with yourself, knowing what you have caused directly. You don't get to turn your head and ignore it; you can finally see clearly. Oh yes, sometimes people go back to Earth, try it again, and fall into the same trap. But sometimes different choices are made that are in keeping with the integrity of the soul and respect for other human beings, other souls.

SL: What would you do if you were here now?

FD: Be retired by the sea. *[laughs]* No. I would be doing peace work and activism, as it is sorely needed now and we are at a transition point. I would read the millions of books available now, and write books expanding on my lofty perspective. *[laughs]* It would be wonderful to enjoy what the modern world has to offer. Travel is so easy; I would do a lot of that. And public speaking and lecturing.

SL: On what?

FD: Peace, love, and rock and roll? Seriously, I would probably work on abolishing slavery again because I feel it is so important, and I am frankly outraged that it has been swept under the rug. After all the work we did, everything we went through—torture and loss of life—there is still so much work left undone.

SL: Do you have any regrets?

FD: None.

SL: Would you have done anything differently?

FD: Maybe lobbied more support. I think I was a little naïve about how much I thought I could accomplish by myself. But I think it was a very good thing at the time, to be optimistic about what I could do.

SL: But you still made a mark on history. The work you did is still appreciated and remembered.

FD: I appreciate that. In my own small way, I guess I did make a contribution. Do I wish I could have wiped out slavery? Yes, I wish I had done more.

SL: But it matters to those you helped.

FD: Yes. I can see that, and I am eternally grateful.

SL: What is your typical day like? Are you working on any projects?

FD: I enjoy my friends and family here. I am in the peace group, along with Abbie Hoffman and others, who are collaborating on this project. I enjoy creating. I am an artist at heart, and I like painting, drawing, and use of color. It relaxes me. Also, I like to tell stories with my art.

SL: What kind of stories?

FD: Stories about history. My hopes and dreams—and mankind's. I hold art shows occasionally so I can display my work.

SL: Are you planning to come back to Earth?

FD: Not anytime soon. It's a bit too much of a cruel world right now, and I don't want to engage with that. I can do more good up here. Maybe when things on Earth come more in line with my utopian vision. *[smiles]* For now, I have no plans to reincarnate.

SL: Thank you. Is there anything else you would like to say?

FD: I want to say thank you, and I hope people listen to our messages. We still have the opportunity to make change. Modern-day slavery is still very much alive and well in all of its forms. See it. Believe it. Know it. Change it. Do not back away, because that is when the actions of others—the most callous—become the most outrageous and dangerous.

Liberty and freedom to all—to all who seek it, love it, and know that it should be so.

Reflections

Frederick Douglass was impressive and inspiring. Even in spirit, there was something very majestic about his presence and in the words he relayed to me. As with Abbie Hoffman, I had not known very much about him when I began this interview. When I finished and looked up some information about him on the Internet, I learned how accomplished he was as a person, diplomat, and public speaker. All of this was particularly surprising given the fact that he was born into slavery, and it had been illegal even to teach him to read as a child. Indeed, there were so many doubters that such an articulate spokesman could have been a slave that in 1845 Douglass began writing his autobiography (which was revised and completed in 1882) titled *Life and Times of Frederick Douglass.* It has since become an American classic.

At this point I had spoken with Ben Franklin, Abbie Hoffman, and Frederick Douglass. They had all discussed social and environmental justice and the importance of taking action. Their messages were wonderful and inspiring, to be sure, but I was beginning to wonder if I was going to have an entire book like this.

Then came Andy Warhol.

CHAPTER 4

ANDY WARHOL

Normally (if such a word can be applied to this book) I write these biographies at the beginning of each chapter. But Andy Warhol preferred to dictate his own:

"I was born Andrew Warhola on August 6, 1928, in Pittsburgh, Pennsylvania. Blah, blah, blah. Here's the good part: I was an avant-garde artist whose art defined my generation. I was famous for my iconic pieces, such as the Campbell's soup cans. I worked with an eclectic mix of media, including hand drawing, painting, printmaking, filmmaking, and photography, and was a pioneer in computer-generated art. My art defied the rules of any particular paradigm, just like me.

"I was shot by a woman named Valerie Solanas in 1968 and almost died. The woman who shot me was one of the people who used to hang out at The Factory, which was my studio. Though I recovered physically, the specter of doom had become my constant companion. I died on February 22, 1987, in New York City, of complications following gallbladder surgery at the age of 58—blah, blah, blah."

I wasn't sure whether Andy's interview was my idea or his. I would think of him and wonder whether he wanted to be interviewed. Then one day an image of his famous soup can appeared to me, and I thought, *There he is!* (Although, strictly speaking, the image I saw was of the Soup Can necklace worn by Dick Shawn's character, "L.S.D.," in the 1968 film *The Producers.*) Then I saw Andy. He looked exactly as he did on Earth during the '80s: pale and thin, silver hair, black-rimmed glasses, dressed in head-to-toe black. Then he disappeared again.

But five days later he reappeared, wearing a crazy green-and-pink wig, and sent me scrambling for some paper to write on.

The Interview

Andy Warhol: The problem with us outsiders is that we even live outside our own relationships. But I was so out I was in!

Susan Lander: Wait! I want to write that down. . . .
Was this interview my idea or yours?

AW: Does it matter? If you want to talk to me, I want to talk to you! *[smiles inscrutably]*
I wish I could have communicated with people over here while I was still on Earth. Now that would have been good fun! Ooh, I would have made great art about that.

SL: From what you were saying, it seemed that you were preoccupied with death and dying while you were here.

AW: That's true. I never felt . . . quite here. Or quite there, as the case may be. Like I might float off the earth, dissolve into a spark, and explode—poof—and be gone in an instant. My greatest fear was oblivion. It was the opposite, the antithesis of everything I wanted—which was permanence.

SL: But now you have that. You're just as famous now as when you were here.

AW: Yes. I loved fame. I still do. It's a way, for a time, to feel like you're part of something bigger than yourself.

SL: I know you had some physical problems. How did you overcome them to become as famous as you did?

AW: Fame is about the spirit, not the body! It doesn't matter what kind of body you have. So many people are afraid to show the world who they are. They think they aren't good enough, or that something is wrong with them. But the truth is, we are who we are, and we came here to Earth to make our mark on the world. That's the point!

SL: Do you have any regrets?

AW: None. Well, getting shot. That scared the daylights out of me. It proved what I'd always feared—that there is such a tenuous, fragile link between life and death, and that thread could snap in an instant. When I was shot, it almost did. That's why I was so afraid to go into the hospital when I was sick at the end with gallbladder problems. I was so afraid that it would be all over. Finito! *The End.*

SL: I read that you'd had gallbladder problems for years and that several doctors agreed that removing it was the only option. Did you just think you would be okay without surgery?

AW: *[dismissive]* Oh, I was never okay, physically, in that lifetime. But I just didn't want it to be real.

SL: Do you mean, you didn't want the pain to mean anything significant or dangerous?

AW: Yes, exactly. But denial didn't exactly win out in the end, did it?

SL: No, I guess it didn't. Did you ever talk about your fears while you were here?

AW: Jed knew. *[He's referring to Jed Johnson, whom he lived with for years.]* Certain people knew. But remember, I didn't want it to be real. Talking about it and dwelling upon it made it real, like it would manifest or something. So I avoided that. Fantasy was where I preferred to live, to retreat into. That was much more comfortable. Much saner. And more real to me, more vibrant and alive, than anything else. It was certainly more interesting than the drudgery and reality of any kind of normal day-to-day life. I tried to avoid that and was quite successful, I think.

SL: Your art was pretty fantastical, too. You took ordinary objects and somehow added fantasy elements to them. Like the soup cans, for example.

AW: That was a paradox, for sure, just like me. I never liked to be pigeonholed or figured out. Sensual but not sexual. Real but a fantasy, you see?

SL: Were you hiding yourself for some reason?

AW: It was part of my mystique, my feminine mystique. *[smiles]* It wasn't my image, those innermost thoughts. In some ways I was really a salesman. I knew how important image was—certainly in my crowd, and certainly at that time. I was part of my own art. I was a whole package. And like a character in a play, I carefully crafted myself.

SL: Looking back, are you glad you did that?

AW: No. Well, yes and no. To the extent I was a package, it was fine and necessary. I was selling myself, the image of myself, and my art. All of that was me. It was all one and the same. Even though I understood its commercial potential, I loved my art. I was driven to produce it. It was the physical manifestation of who I was and what I wanted to present to the world.

SL: We've spent a lot of time talking about your physical issues, and you talked about feeling like an outsider. If you hadn't had physical illnesses and felt like an outsider, do you think your art would have been different?

AW: *[laughs]* One hundred percent, I think. My art was me, a snapshot in the moment.

SL: If you hadn't "carefully crafted" yourself, as you said, do you think your life and relationships would have been better?

AW: I liked my life just fine, thanks! It was fun. Exciting. Glamorous. It worked for me. I was enormously wealthy. Afraid I would lose that, but I enjoyed it. If people knew the real me—morose, brooding, ill, full of fears—that wouldn't have been much fun, would it? It wouldn't have sold many paintings. "Oh, here's a depressed guy selling a painting of a soup can. No, thank you, weird guy." It wouldn't have sold back then. Not in the era of glamour, good times, excess, and my favorite club, Studio 54. It was all fantasy and light escapism. I was just good at tapping into the vibe of the moment, encapsulating it, and selling it. Making money from it. My gift, I guess.

SL: You said in an interview that you didn't believe in romance. Is that still true? Or was that even true then?

AW: Now you're starting to understand me. Now I believe in love. True, soul-mate love.

SL: Do you have a soul mate on the Other Side?

AW: Yes.

SL: I'm seeing a woman with you . . .

AW: She likes to think so.

SL: Was Jed Johnson, the man you lived with, your soul mate?

AW: Of a sort, yes. I loved him. I was devastated when he left. I did not want to go on. It was my fault. I could have done things differently, with him at least. I could have been more real with him, paid more attention to him. He deserved that. He was real, and I wasn't. Not really. But when it comes right down to it, I don't think I was really capable of it at the time. Because, like I said, outsiders even live outside of their own relationships. But he is here on the Other Side now. He knows that I am sorry and that I still love him to this day. He is a great man. Loyal. He deserves great happiness, and I wish him that.

SL: I read that your mom passed, so she's on the Other Side, too.

AW: Yes, thank God for that. We are great friends. I see her every day.
There are some other people I want to acknowledge who were important to me: Edie Sedgwick, Dennis Hopper, Debbie Harry, Madonna, and my brothers. I also want to acknowledge Pittsburgh, my beautiful hometown.

SL: What do you do on the Other Side for fun?

AW: Paint. I'm still an artist. Still introspective. I spend a lot of time alone now, and I enjoy that. I needed a rest big-time. I really did live my life to the fullest. I'm happy I did that, and happy I was successful at the game of life.

SL: What do you think about your art shows that are now at the Smithsonian and about your art living on?

AW: Wasn't how I would arrange the installations . . . *[huge smile]* Are you kidding? I love it! I'm still me. Still grandstanding after all these years from the great beyond. May it keep happening, please! I love immortality. It's like a great cosmic joke somehow. Isn't living forever the ultimate fantasy? And I get to do that! The universe is letting me have my way with everyone one last time.

SL: I believe that we plan many of the major events in our lives before we come to Earth in order to learn. Would you agree with that?

AW: Yes, I would. With a certain amount of randomness thrown in.

SL: What was the big life lesson you were supposed to work on here?

AW: Humility! Just kidding. Self-acceptance. Self-love.

SL: Was the shooting planned before you came to Earth?

AW: Yes, it was a distinct possibility.

SL: What was the purpose?

AW: Again, self-acceptance and self-love. Anytime you have to deal with physical or emotional difficulties, it's an invitation to love and accept yourself as you are in the moment. Humans are prone to perfectionism, so anytime we are sick or injured or disabled or what have you, we can be very judgmental and harsh with ourselves. But these are all opportunities to get past these judgments. The happier you are with yourself, the happier you'll be with your life, and you will make better choices, too.

SL: Do you have any advice you would give to young artists?

AW: Give the people what they want, but be true to yourself. That way you can't lose.

SL: Do you have any grand messages to humanity?

AW: Don't take yourselves too seriously. See the fun and the beauty in everyday life. And be real when it counts.

SL: I once heard that you wanted only the word *figment* to be on your tombstone. Would that still be true, or would you change it?

AW: Good question, especially when answered from the Other Side. I think it would be blank.

SL: Meaning?

AW: Here one minute, gone the next.

SL: One final question. What was your favorite work of art?

AW: Me!

SL: Thank you so much.

AW: My pleasure. May peace be with you, my child. Love, peace, and blessings to you all.

[He shows me two images: (1) a painting of the Last Supper and other religious art references, and I'm hearing tabula rasa, *which means "blank slate," and (2) a graphic painting of a spoon filled with sugar in red and white.]*

SL: Andy, is the spoonful of sugar a new work of art?

[He smiles. Inscrutable as always.]

Reflections

Speaking with Andy Warhol was an adventure. He was intense and fun, and his answers were unpredictable. He even had a few surprises up his sleeve at the end of the interview, showing me those images—one of which seems to be a painting that, to my knowledge, doesn't exist on Earth.

Following the interview, I did some Internet research. The first thing I discovered was that his final series of paintings, completed in 1986, consisted of dozens of variations of da Vinci's famous painting *The Last Supper.* There was a black-light version, a camouflage version, and versions that included commercial logos from products such as potato chips and cigarettes. I then searched for works with that image of the spoonful of sugar, but was unable to locate any.

Finally, I looked up Jed Johnson, Andy's companion and rumored romantic partner. I learned that he had been an interior decorator for many celebrities. Tragically, he was on board TWA Flight 800, which exploded shortly after takeoff on July 17, 1996. None of the 230 passengers survived.

Those wishing to learn more about Andy Warhol may be interested in the book *The Andy Warhol Diaries.* Every day, from 1976 to shortly before his death in 1987, Andy narrated a diary entry to his secretary, Pat Hackett. She collected 20,000 pages of entries, which she then edited to a manageable size and published in 1989.

Once my interview with Andy Warhol was finished, I began the now-familiar guessing game of "Who's next?" Let's face it, it's pretty hard to top Andy Warhol for iconic power. However, next up was Farrah Fawcett, who'd been immortalized in two Andy Warhol silk-screen portraits in 1980.

CHAPTER 5

FARRAH FAWCETT

When Farrah Fawcett came to visit, the first image I received was a flash of her big, beautiful smile—it was like a thousand-watt flashbulb lighting up. Then I saw her. She looked gorgeous and appeared to be about 30 years old. She had the most beautiful energy! So gentle and fawn-like, she felt sweet, warm, kind, empathetic, honest, and unselfconscious. Her manner was friendly and easygoing, and when she began talking, she had a slight Southern accent—the phrase "all peaches and cream" comes to mind. I could feel that Hollywood life and being in the limelight had been hard for her. Part of her just wanted peace and quiet, but she was driven to that life by fate, faith, and destiny.

Farrah was born on February 2, 1947, in Corpus Christi, Texas. She was an internationally successful TV and film star, nominated for multiple Golden Globe and Emmy awards. She is especially known for her role in the 1970s TV series *Charlie's Angels,* as well as her trendsetting flip hairstyle and the iconic poster of her in a red swimsuit that sold millions of copies. She often took on difficult subjects in her acting, such as domestic violence. One notable role was in the TV movie *The Burning Bed,* based on the true story of a woman who killed her abusive husband. It was the first TV movie to display a hotline when it aired, to help victims of domestic violence.

Farrah had two notable romantic partners, both of whom are mentioned in this interview. She was married to actor Lee Majors from 1973 to 1982; he is perhaps best known for his role as Colonel Steve Austin in the 1970s TV series *The Six Million Dollar Man*. But her longest romantic involvement by far was with actor Ryan O'Neal; their on-and-off relationship spanned three decades. They had one son, Redmond O'Neal. In 2012, Ryan published an intimate memoir in which he documents their deeply passionate but sometimes stormy relationship, titled *Both of Us: My Life with Farrah*.

Following Farrah's diagnosis with anal cancer in 2006, she documented her journey and her relationship with O'Neal in the films *A Wing & a Prayer: Farrah's Fight for Life* and *Farrah's Story*. He was with her when she lost her battle with cancer on June 25, 2009, in Santa Monica, California, at the age of 62.

The Interview

Susan Lander: Hi, Farrah! It's so nice to meet you. What would you like to talk about?

Farrah Fawcett: I would like to talk about the meaning of illness, personal responsibility and potential, love in all its forms, children, and the pain of not finishing what we came here to do.

SL: I followed what you went through with cancer. You were very brave.

FF: I don't think it was bravery. I just fought in the worst way. I didn't want to leave, and I was so worried about Ryan and my son. *[She shows me an image of Ryan O'Neal crying.]* I don't know if that makes me brave or a control freak.

SL: How did you meet Ryan?

FF: We traveled in similar circles. Ryan is my soul mate, so we were drawn to each other right away.

SL: I'd like to ask you some questions about your career. Do you think you were limited by typecasting in the roles you were offered?

FF: Hollywood tried to typecast me both as a "bimbo" and a "victim," but I chose projects based on what my heart told me to do. I was driven to take certain roles because I knew I was here for a greater purpose. I knew that I had center stage and that I could use it to make a difference, for better or for worse. When it comes down to it, we all have personal responsibility for the choices we make.

SL: It seems in Hollywood that there are two extremes: victims who have no power, and bimbos who have all the power and are invincible.

FF: Grace. What they are missing is grace—the grace of the person's humanity. I always tried to portray the person's essential humanity, heart, and grace.

SL: Why do you think you were so successful as an actor?

FF: The reason I was successful is because I was willing to plumb the depths. Actors who are not willing to look at their dark sides and the potential ugliness of themselves and humanity have only half the equation. They are shortchanging themselves and the audience, and are missing out on their own genius and what they have to offer to themselves and the world. Audiences know when you are telling the truth.

If I could give actors one piece of advice, it is to be the truth and be your truth always—you have nothing to lose and everything to gain. It's a win-win, and it is basic. This is the difference between what makes one a star (although I hesitate to use that word) or not. Charisma is important, but being authentic is the essential ingredient that is often missing.

Honesty in the character is everything, regardless of how much you identify with the character. Just be as honest as you can. Get out of your head and into your heart. I always tried to do that. Sometimes I succeeded, sometimes not, but I knew I was on the right track when I did that. Don't hold back. Don't be afraid.

SL: What do you feel you gave the world through your talents?

FF: Insight, sympathy, and empathy. Greater understanding of those in need and those in pain. We need to help them. Don't turn your face away. We can all do so much to alleviate the suffering of those victimized by others and by society. It doesn't take much. A kind word goes a long way, especially if someone is being bullied. Small financial and material contributions are also really important; donating clothes that you don't need is a perfect example. You can be the critical difference between life and death for someone in need. It's your choice.

SL: What do you think was your finest career success?

FF: *Burning Bed.* It was about domestic violence. I tried to raise it to the next level and not have it be just a "victim movie." In large part, I think I succeeded.

SL: What was your finest personal success?

FF: How do you really separate the personal and professional, at least careerwise? I am what I did. I did what I am.

SL: I can see that.

FF: But personally, my greatest success is my son, Redmond. I love him so much! He is a good boy, a good kid. He does struggle, though. He's just had a very hard path dealing with addiction, and it doesn't help that he's in the public eye. But I can help him from here now. That is a good thing.

SL: How?

FF: I can talk to him, be with him. Give him motivation to stay on track. Clean and sober, you know. So he is really my greatest success.

SL: Your relationship with Ryan O'Neal? Can I ask?

FF: I knew you were going to ask that. Aah . . . people are so curious. It was hard, easy, love. Confusing. Elevating. At times I didn't understand it. At other times I understood it perfectly. I miss him. I don't like being without him on a daily basis. What can I say? The path, wants, and needs of the heart are mysterious.

SL: It was volatile, wasn't it?

FF: Yes. We didn't get along all that well. We fought, and of course that was in the public eye, too. But that's over now, and what's left is love. The shining, effervescent moments. He was there until the end. I visit him at night, in his dreams. I know he misses me. It was magical, in its own way.

SL: Thank you for sharing that. I know people are interested.

FF: This is not for them. This is for him so he knows I'm here, I'm fine, and I will love him always and forever.

SL: Thank you. How did this life help you move forward in your development?

FF: It helped me move forward, but I feel like I only got halfway there. I was cut off by illness and disease. Rats! I was so disappointed when I lost that fight and had to return Home unfinished.

SL: What had you come to Earth to work on, that you were "halfway there"?

FF: Educating the public about abusive relationships. The public got to see it playing out in various ways—personal and professional—in my life and career.

SL: Are you referring to a relationship or incident in particular?

FF: I don't need to spell it out. My life was my life, and really, it's all been said. The memoirs have been written and filmed. The articles have been published. What is important is the message that I hope people learned from my experiences and from the roles that I played. It is important that we always treat each other with love and respect. Violence is never okay, never a solution. It violates everything we hold precious, spiritually, as souls. There is always another way rather than to approach another person with violence, abuse, or lack of kindness.

SL: So you came here to work on love, family, and respect, and to teach others about it?

FF: Yes, and to be a public figure around these issues. Natch. A leader type, if you will.

SL: So you did that.

FF: Yes, I guess I did. *[smiles]* Thank you. I still feel a bit unfinished about it. I wish I'd had longer. In some ways, I feel I was just hitting my stride, my full power. The illness and that fight finally led me there.

SL: Are you saying that your illness made you stronger?

FF: Yes, without a doubt. A paradox, isn't it? While I was getting weaker, my soul was getting stronger. It made me really understand more about how precious life is, and how suddenly and easily it can be taken away. *[I can see and hear her snapping her fingers.]* I was here and then—poof! Gone the next minute. I feel like it all happened so fast at the end. I lost the body part of the fight, but I guess my soul won.

SL: So if you could give people one sage piece of wisdom that you learned from everything in this lifetime, what would it be?

FF: Enjoy the ride, baby, because it will be over before you know it. Every moment is precious. Every relationship is special. Love it all. Honor it all. Respect it all. Have fun. Play. Eat. Enjoy the good things and the pleasures. But it's really important to keep a good perspective on the challenging parts, because that's how you learn and grow. It sounds like a cliché, but it's really to your advantage.

This is no dress rehearsal; this is the real deal. Every day you're given opportunities to become a better person, and every day you're given opportunities to make the best choices possible. Take them, please, before it's too late. If you make a choice you don't like, or you think you can do better, you get the chance to redo it. Did you miss an opportunity? Take it the next time. There is great power in this, and the opportunity for great mastery, as practice makes perfect. Make the choice now to be your best self. It really is up to you. Imagine looking down at your life from a higher perspective. How do you want the story of your life to read? What changes are needed to give you that happy ending? Work toward those changes now.

SL: Thank you. Are you planning to come back?

FF: Maybe in a little while; I'm taking a rest. That was an intense life, with a rough ending. A good life, but still, I am enjoying the break.

SL: What's your favorite thing to do on the Other Side?

FF: Lots of things: Small parties to catch up with friends. Reading, resting, picnics, singing, making music. Hanging with "my cats." *[I'm seeing a tiger cat.]* Painting. *[I'm seeing a watercolor painting of a sailboat in very blue water.]* Sailing. Acting in a play in a coliseum.

SL: What is the play about?

FF: It's Shakespeare, *A Midsummer Night's Dream*. I'm doing it for fun. I don't think I really appreciated Shakespeare before. It's simple in that it gets to the heart of the characters, but complex in that you have to really study it to get to the meaning.

I've also been thinking about my last life, and what I might have done differently.

SL: What would you have done differently? Do you have any regrets?

FF: Not exactly. I wish that I had insisted on respect at all times in all of my relationships, all of my contracts, and all of my interactions. There was a time when I didn't think I deserved respect. On one level I got that I did, but I was too afraid to stand up for myself. But I deserve respect; we all do. That is fundamental.

I wish that people understood that they are beautiful, holy, and Divine, and that they are worthy of respect just because of that. People don't need to be anything else or do anything else to be worthy of respect.

SL: Why is there suffering and poverty on Earth?

FF: To learn. To give us the opportunity to change. To change the way we see people who are different from us. To change the way we treat people, and to make a difference for those in need. Earth is a very tough place. So many difficult problems, so much pain. But can't you see, this gives us so many opportunities to act and to be one of those people who actually make change. I urge you to seize these opportunities before it's too late.

SL: Too late?

FF: Before you have to leave. There is nothing worse than having to leave before you feel you're finished. Trust me, I know. It is very frustrating. So take your time when it is given to you.

SL: What is wonderful about the world that we don't appreciate?

FF: The animals. Even the bugs. It is all so amazing, the variety of life that is on Earth. It's so magical that people walk into (and out of) our lives all the time? So many opportunities to see or do something good every day, and people overlook them. Don't forget to smile at people—even strangers. It can make their day.

SL: What would you like to be remembered for?

FF: Insight. Honesty. Vulnerability. Conviction. I followed my path from the heart. Whatever else people may say, that I did! I am proud of myself for that. I didn't care so much what people thought. I just followed the beat of my "inner drummer" and walked that path.

But I still feel like I only got halfway down that path. I had more to say, and I wanted to make sure people heard me, so this is one of the main reasons I'm doing this interview.

SL: What else would you like to say?

FF: That I love you, all of you. And thank you—I couldn't have done what I came here to do without you. You catapulted me to fame. I felt your love and support and encouragement, and I felt that you wanted me to succeed. I felt how you shared my successes and pain and disappointments, especially in my personal life. You wouldn't believe how many people wrote me personal letters of encouragement and shared their experiences. It kept me going through the dark times—through the pain, violence, disappointments, and addictions. It was hard to go through that while I was in the public eye. It was a little embarrassing. But more than anything, I felt your acceptance, support, and unconditional love.

To all of you who supported me, I wish I could thank you individually here. But I can't. Just know I hold each and every one of you near and dear to my heart. I love you, and I thank you. It has been a wild ride, and I am fine. I am free.

SL: I just have a couple of final questions. I want to ask you about *Charlie's Angels*.

FF: *[laughs]* I knew you were going to ask me that. It was fun. I was so afraid of getting typecast, though, and I knew that was a potential risk. But the show launched me to stardom and gave me the opportunity to do more important work. It was so nice to work with all those women: Jaclyn Smith, Kate Jackson, and Cheryl Ladd, who essentially took over my role. Fierce, amazing women, all.

Tell them I love them and miss them. All was not always perfect, but let bygones be bygones. Petty stuff is just petty stuff, and over here I see clearly. It is so much easier to see clearly when the ego-mind is removed.

SL: One more question: How did you feel about your physical beauty?

FF: I liked the way I looked. It helped get me attention, and it was a stepping-stone. Beauty is only skin-deep, of course. True beauty is inside and radiates out.

One more thing: to Lee Majors, I'm thinking of you and wanted to say hello and send my love. You were very significant to me in many ways.

SL: Thank you for sharing so much in this interview.

FF: Thank you for giving me the opportunity for some more closure.

I am sending you all love and a million blessings, straight from my little heart! I love you, and please be all that you can be—now!

Reflections

I loved connecting with Farrah and her energy so much that I didn't want the interview to end! Sadly, I knew that I had to let her go. That is part of my journey and responsibility as a medium. We get to glimpse the Other Side, bask in its amazing energy, and connect with those who are there, but we must always let go. We still have to live on Earth.

In one of the many synchronicities surrounding this book, I was surprised to learn during the writing of these Reflections that Ryan O'Neal was in the middle of a legal trial with the University of Texas at Austin over an Andy Warhol portrait of Farrah! Farrah had bequeathed her art collection to the university, which included one of two famous portraits that Warhol had created of her in 1980. In dispute was the ownership of the second Andy Warhol portrait. O'Neal cherished this portrait, and the jury ultimately decided that he could keep it. After I read about the jury verdict, I saw Farrah smiling.

My next visit was from another woman who made a big difference with a soft touch (and a sewing needle), Betsy Ross.

CHAPTER 6

BETSY ROSS

At this point in the interview sessions, I was starting to put together a list of spirits I thought might be coming to talk with me, and Betsy Ross was one of them.

Born Elizabeth Griscom on January 1, 1752, in Philadelphia, Pennsylvania, Betsy was trained as an upholsterer, which in colonial times involved all types of sewing, including flag making. She is credited with sewing the first American flag at the request of George Washington, Robert Morris, and George Ross. Known as the "Stars and Stripes," the flag featured a circle of 13 five-pointed stars, symbolizing the unity of the original 13 colonies that had severed ties with Britain, and was adopted by the Continental Congress in 1777.

Betsy died on January 30, 1836, in Philadelphia at the age of 84. According to her, her cause of death was "something about the lungs. I think you call it pneumonia, consumption, or tuberculosis. Natural causes, though. Everybody has to die of something."

On the day I saw her, Betsy announced herself by showing me an image of a colonial-era woman holding the first American flag. She was a pretty, delicate woman, a little curvy, with pale skin, brown eyes, and a pointy nose. She looked old-fashioned in her long yellow dress with white trim, complete with a very full petticoat and ruffled white cap. When she showed me an image of the Betsy Ross House in Philadelphia, a place I had visited many times as a child, I realized who she was and was excited by the prospect of talking with her. Like her friend and fellow revolutionary, Ben Franklin, Betsy is a much-admired folk hero to us Philadelphians.

As she told me what she was planning to say, I kept asking, "Are you sure? Are you sure?" She knew it was going to really surprise people, and, oh yes, she was sure.

Following is the beautiful statement that Betsy read to me, which she had prepared on the Other Side. It came in so quickly (in under ten minutes) that I had a hard time writing fast enough to keep up with her. I didn't want to miss a word of it! After her rather amazing posthumous revelation, I followed up with some questions.

The Interview

Betsy Ross: I am gay. And I fly the flag of pride and liberty for all of us. Don't you see, it isn't just for you, or you, or you? It is for all of us.

We came to America to escape the tyrannical rule in England, where our lives were dictated, our destinies were dictated. Please do not let our hard work be for naught. We are in real danger of taking that path.

Freedom is paramount. And I still fly that flag for all of us. For I believe in it wholeheartedly. Do not let it slip backward, for it is a very slippery slope indeed—like a mudslide, until there is nothing left under our feet to hold us up. Together we really can rise up, and be all that we can be, in liberty and freedom. Or we can fall together and go back into history, to a time when our freedom and our destiny as a nation were not assured.

I am gay, you see. And I will still fly the flag of liberty and freedom for us all. I beg of you, think back to what that really means. We have come so far—too far to step backward into a time when people who were different were pilloried, tortured, executed, or excluded just because they did not agree with those in power. Just because they had a secret. Or just because they were different.

Secrets are painful. Secrets are deadly. Secrets prevent people from manifesting their destiny. I beg of you, take heed. See what kind of world you are creating again with your restrictions that are ever increasing. You must have faith that being who you are is enough; you do not need to make everyone else that way to give the world its order. I understand why—it is easier to live in a world that is black-and-white. I urge you to explore the gray. You may even like it. For there is such danger inherent in the road we are currently traveling.

Freedom is not just an ideal. Freedom is part of our foundation as a country. Take that away, and there is nothing left to stand on.

Let history record this.

Susan Lander: Why did you want to come out as gay now, after all this time?

BR: I am speaking out now as a revolutionary act! I felt it was time, and I no longer wanted to carry this secret. Enough of that! No one can hurt me now. Indeed, I regret that I couldn't be open at the time and am grateful for this opportunity to set the record straight. Thank you.

I want history to reflect accurately who I was, what I was, all I was. I want it to reflect my truth, and I want you all to hear it. No more hiding anymore; I am clearing the record.

It is so ironic; I was thought of as a revolutionary, but I did not feel the freedom to be who I was. It was too dangerous.

SL: Did you have a girlfriend?

BR: Yes. I was part of an underground gay and lesbian community in Philadelphia. We knew each other, where we were. But it was very covert, for sure. The stakes were very high.

SL: What would have happened if the truth had come out?

BR: Imprisonment, death, torture, ostracism. So we kept it secret, and expressed our love in private. But aah . . . the heart wants what it wants. We are, ultimately, who we are. And love is love. It truly has no boundaries. That is its beauty and its essence. No matter what anyone tries to say to the contrary, one can't control it when it comes to matters of the heart.

SL: Why did you want to participate in this project and give an interview?

BR: I am aware of the ultrapolarized political agendas that I feel are leading us down the wrong path. I urge people to take a step back and look at the bigger picture of suppression of liberty and freedom that is running rampant in today's society. The erosion of free speech, free love, autonomy, and the equal rights of women and others. Our right to live out our lives in freedom, as long as we don't hurt anyone. These are all in the greatest jeopardy.

There is another dimension to this as well. Suppression limits us—our ability to create, achieve, and grow during our lifetimes and overall as souls. It is stifling and limiting in ways that are not just superficial. It runs very deep.

SL: Some people say you didn't sew the flag. Is that true?

BR: *[laughing]* It was a partial fabrication!

Reflections

When Betsy answered my last question, I saw a flash of Ben Franklin, and I just knew that he had something to do with that last line! It was just like his sense of humor, and he was very famous for his puns. I asked Betsy for clarification of that statement, and she said that while she did not design the flag herself, she "did have a hand in sewing it."

Given her revelation that she is gay, I looked up information on her marital status while she lived on Earth. I learned that she'd had three husbands: John Ross (m. 1773–1776), who died while serving in the militia; Joseph Ashburn (m. 1777–1782), a sea captain who died in England as a prisoner of war, and with whom she had two children; and John Claypoole (m. 1783–1817), who died of illness, and with whom she had five children.

When I questioned her about her marriages, she acknowledged that she loved and cared very much for her husbands, then added: "Those were tough times, especially for women. It was very hard, if not impossible, for women to support themselves. Women married for many reasons, including economic and physical security. Back then, it was about survival. But I was alone a lot, and had plenty of time for female companionship. That was what really touched my heart."

My next visitor moves us even further back in time and history: to the reign of King Charlemagne.

———————

CHAPTER 7

KING CHARLEMAGNE

I'd describe this man as a "handsome devil." Not to suggest that Charlemagne is a devil! But even in spirit, I could sense his power and charisma, as well as his humor. When he appeared to me, he was blond with blue-gray eyes and a mustache, and wearing a velvety burgundy tunic with gold trim and cream hose. It was easy to see why he was so popular with the ladies (he had five wives, several concubines, and at least 18 children). He wasn't rough at all, kind of refined in a way, and had some softness to his energy. I'd say he looked and felt like a hunky, 8th-century version of Bill Clinton!

King Charlemagne, Charles I, was also known to his contemporaries as *Carolus Magnus* ("Charles the Great") and *Europae pater* ("father of Europe"). He was born circa A.D. 742 in what is now Belgium. Charlemagne reigned as king of the Franks from 768, king of the Lombards from 774, and emperor from 800 until his death in 814. He was a brilliant military leader and politician. He was deeply connected to the Christian church, and crowned emperor by Pope Leo III. He was smart, athletic, courageous, and well liked and respected.

During his reign, he expanded his kingdom to include most of Western Europe. He was associated with honoring customs and tradition, but he also instituted many internal and cultural reforms, including the revival of art, religion, education, and law. This ultimately resulted in establishing uniformity across the land and a central authority. However, his military campaigns were brutal and involved mass killings, pillaging, and forcible conversions to Christianity under penalty of death. It is impossible to summarize the reign of Charlemagne and the impact he had in a few lines, but one thing is certain: his decisions, actions, social and economic programs, and military campaigns played a profound role in shaping history.

He died on January 28, 814, in Aachen, Austrasia (what is now Germany), at approximately age 71. As to his cause of death, he said, "It doesn't matter. I didn't want to go yet; I wanted to reign another 65 years, at least. I felt sometimes that I wasn't subject to human limitations. But in the end, I was just as vulnerable to death as anyone else."

The Interview

Susan Lander: During your reign as king, you greatly expanded your territory. But I understand that this included forcibly converting the Saxons to Christianity under penalty of death. How can you reconcile being a good Christian with participating in the death and destruction that comes with war?

Charlemagne: In the rule book of how you do things on this planet, if you want something, you either get it or take it forcibly. It was what we knew. And we were only doing what one did in these situations. I realize that it may be hard to understand, but to my soldiers and me, it was not personal. It was stylized, ritualized, and choreographed—it was "the Game." It was a dance, a show. It is not an accident that it is called the "theater" of war.

This gave war a depersonalized aspect. There was no personal responsibility, only collective responsibility, and therefore collective personal and emotional separation from our enemies. We divorced ourselves from the personal aspects of it, for to connect personally would mean certain death. It was not "me versus them," but "us versus them." It sounds cruel and harsh, but our opponents were faceless and symbolic of that which must be ended, the situation that must be corrected. It was all about an allegiance to something greater than ourselves.

SL: Did you feel you had to justify it at the moment?

C: Oh no. It was what had to be done. I never gave that a second thought. As long as I functioned within the rules, I was protected and on the path of the righteous. I knew the parameters and stayed within them. I felt as if I was participating in my own enlightenment. At least that's how I saw it then.

SL: From your current perspective, can you still reconcile mass killing or genocide with being a good person?

C: I can't now. They were two separate, completely compartmentalized parts of my life back then. But as I said, if you functioned within the rules, you remained a good person. It was just another route to enlightenment. A high route, actually. This was true of wars but also all of the other aspects of one's life, too. For example, it was acceptable to have many wives and mistresses. *[laughs]*
Don't underestimate the impact of societal mores on behavior and beliefs. What is considered ethical now may not be considered ethical in the future, and vice versa. When I was on Earth, I felt that I was staying within the societally, culturally approved rules. That was my protection.

SL: Protection from what?

C: From burning in the eternal fires of hell. From death. From straying from the path of the righteous.

SL: Is there a hell?

C: Not really. *[smiles]* Just ones of our own making. We are all good at that. There are so many gifts surrounding us and within us, bestowed upon us from God. If we could only see or tap into that, our lives would be so much easier. It really can offer us insulation from the trials and tribulations of our lives on Earth.

SL: Does being a good person mean something different to you now?

C: Now I would definitely hold myself to a higher ethical standard—more of a universal ethical standard. But remember, Earth-consciousness was not the same back then as it is today.

SL: Do you feel bad about what you did back then? After all, you were a leader.

C: Being a leader was my job. I wish we had known that there was another way. But back then, it was the way things were done. Maybe it was something I could or should have thought about as a leader. Maybe I could have made different choices that would have led to different outcomes, but I didn't know any better.

From my perspective now, I believe in nonviolent confrontations and problem solving with words, not swords or catapults. I believe in repairing conflicts through diplomacy. But if I came back, who knows whether I would do anything differently at all? Maybe yes, maybe no. I just don't know.

I am a warrior and a soldier. I still feel that way. I still like the idea of creating societal change. I would hope that if given the chance, I would do something different—something grand and forward thinking, or at least forward leaning. But again, I just don't know. I haven't been on Earth in a very, very long time—over a thousand of your Earth years. I'm not sure how I would respond to all the stimuli, all the choices, all the options. It is a very complex world you live in today, much more so than when I lived on Earth. I still maintain those sensibilities and that perspective, in a way.

SL: What way?

C: I'm kind of old-fashioned and a relic in some ways, I think.

SL: In what ways?

C: I memorized those old rule books very well. *[smiles]*

SL: But I recall reading that you did not have a formal education when you were here as Charlemagne!

C: That's true, but I possessed an extremely sharp memory. And I was a strong leader.

I feel like some of my ideas about male-female relationships and war and the way things should be done are still stuck in the past. I was very masculine in that lifetime, and I still feel that way. I do not have that softer female energy and spirit.

SL: Give me one example of an idea you have that is "stuck in the past."

C: That males are meant to be dominant and go out and fight wars, and women stay home and take care of the children and don't fight. And males can have mistresses, and women can't. Have affairs, I mean. *[smiles]* I know that is incredibly dated and not fair, really, but I am a relic in that way. I try to fight these outmoded ideas within myself, with varying degrees of success. It is like I haven't really unlearned it on some level. But I am working on it. We all have these rule books, these internal scripts that we learned. I would like to get past this. Maybe next time. *[smiles]*

SL: Are you planning to come back to Earth?

C: Not right now. But this is making me think about it. Maybe it will be time soon.

SL: If you come back, what would you want to be?

C: A warrior, of course! Going on another crusade to change the world.

SL: Maybe you could come back as a female this time, so you can learn a different perspective.

C: Maybe I would. *[smiles]*

SL: Did you have any other lifetimes on Earth since your lifetime as Charlemagne?

C: One—it seems irrelevant when compared to my Charlemagne lifetime. I was a low-ranking warrior in the geographical boundaries of what is now Scotland. I did not accomplish what I came here to do.

SL: Which was?

C: To change the world, of course. But I was killed and taken early from that life. It was so disappointing. I was a midlevel noble-man, a landowner and a royal, but I never excelled at my military career. I did not get as far as I would have liked in that lifetime. Oh well, you win some and you lose some.

SL: During the lifetime that you were King Charlemagne, what was it like to be you?

C: Fun, but also tremendously burdensome. I felt a crushing weight of responsibility upon my shoulders to all of my loyal subjects and my family. I felt like I owed them something—peace, safety, security, and protection. It was my responsibility, and I tried to live up to that, to not disappoint them. I felt it was my job and my moral responsibility back then. I think I was successful.

SL: What was your least favorite quality about yourself?

C: Ego. Pride. Boastfulness.

SL: What was your favorite quality?

C: Steadfastness and confidence.

SL: In your abilities?

C: Yes, but about everything, in the way I conducted all aspects of my life. Home life, husband, lover, friend, confidant.

SL: Did you ever feel fear?

C: I tried not to. I pushed those feelings away and replaced them with reaffirmations of faith that all was what it should be for me. I had faith in that. I acted from my gut, from feelings and instinct, and tried not to question things too much. That would have been potentially deadly for me, both literally and figuratively.

A good leader should never show a lack of confidence. We have to project a sense of inner faith, calmness, and assuredness that we know what we're doing! We have to take action as if we know what we're doing—there is no room for weakness or vacillating. It instills others' faith in you, and lets them have confidence in you as their leader. It gives them peace, a feeling of comfort and security that you are taking care of them and they will be safe. A good leader will allow them this and knows they need this from him.

SL: But there aren't any guarantees. Don't you think people know this?

C: Yes. But it is part of the mass illusion or mass delusion. I don't mean that people are ignorant. It's just that we all participate in this together to make ourselves feel safe in an unsafe world, a world full of variables and unknowns. It is okay for us to comfort each other in this way. It is part of the game of Earth.

SL: What do you think made you a great leader?

C: Steadfastness. I loved my royal subjects. They were like my children to me. I held them in the highest esteem and regard. I wanted to protect them, take care of them, and make them safe.

I liked the life of a king. It had so many rewards. I was comfortable and surrounded by nice things: huge castles, beautiful women, money, power, good food, and options—at least more than most. I had many beautiful children whom I loved and who brought me great joy. I did not lack for anything.

But make no mistake: I felt the crushing weight of responsibility upon my shoulders. It was a great burden to bear and was my constant companion. The people's confidence in me made it so. I will never forget that or forgive it. It was hard and it drove me, and it could be relentless. I am grateful for the confidence they had in me. I can still feel it to this day. It contributed to who I am and makes me strong.

From a spiritual perspective, taking on the role of someone in such power and authority is a huge lesson. Out of my many lives, this one affected me the most.

SL: Why do you think that is?

C: Because of my level of responsibility for others. Because I was a change agent and a catalyst of change for others on such a massive scale. It is the highest calling and the most intense lesson. When you're in it, you feel the immense responsibility, the gravitas.

And now, looking back from this perspective, I can really see how much the life I elected to live changed the lives of untold millions of souls and their progeny. That is huge and that is grave, and it must never be overlooked or disrespected. Every soul deserves enormous respect individually and collectively, just for being who they are—holy and Divine. We are all holy and Divine, and we are all in this together.

SL: Do you still feel a connection to Christianity?

C: Christianity and Christ as the Son of God will always hold a special place in my heart. Up here, people's religious beliefs, thoughts, and prayers are as varied as they are on Earth. Indeed, that is *why* they are so varied on Earth! People carry these notions with them regardless of whether they are on Earth or on the Other Side, and each is just a different way to view the God force. People have their own images and interpretations of what the God force looks like, and what it means for them individually. It colors how they see the world around them. It's as diverse as we are as individuals, and there's nothing wrong with that. It will be this way by necessity.

SL: While you were here, you placed a high priority on converting people to Christianity. How do you feel about that now?

C: It was a mistake. I believe people should have a choice in their beliefs. You cannot change what is in their hearts or force a change in their beliefs. You must remember that at the time I was on a mission. I thought a united front was best, and I thought this would "save" everyone. Remember that I thought this was part of the path to enlightenment. It was my job to take care of and protect everyone, and this fit in perfectly with my worldview at the time. It was quite simplistic, as I said, and naïve, but it was just part of the times. A cultural snapshot in history. Religion as salvation.

From my perspective now, I do not believe religion can save anyone, but it can give you a feeling of peace, safety, comfort, and belonging. It is somehow in our wiring to seek that as souls, and we are drawn to that. It is okay to have these feelings. It is okay to want these things. We are beings of love at our essence, so it is natural that we seek these warm feelings.

Sometimes we are misguided as to where we place our faith. Sometimes not. But try always to stay within your moral center, where your integrity lies. Be who you are. Respect yourself and others. And you will be okay, you will grow and prosper as a soul. You can come down to Earth if you want to accelerate the learning process. Otherwise you will end up like me—an old man who still sees the honor in fighting a good, fair war, and still thinks women should stay home with the babies and raise the families while the husbands go off to war or off to work. It's just a different use of their myriad talents. I'm just being honest. But I know I'm going to catch hell for that one. I'd better not go home tonight. *[smiles]*

SL: Did you enjoy being dubbed "Charles the Great"?

C: *[laughing]* It was rather grand, wasn't it? It made me feel so. Words are so powerful! The name was part of the pomp and circumstance of the moment. It was the way things were done. It seems incredibly archaic at the moment, though, doesn't it? I was Charles the Great? Or even worse, part of me still feels like I'm Charles the Great? Such a relic.

SL: What was it like to be you in that moment?"

C: It's good to be the king. *[laughs]* But seriously, I like to think of all the good I did. Even if I could occasionally be a little off in my ideals, I like to think I tried. And I did exactly what I came to Earth to do. So I'm happy; I lived from my moral center and ideals. I can rest easy.

SL: Do you have any advice for our countries' leaders today?

C: Let the people know you are there for them, for that is why they put you in a position of power. Do not forget this piece of it. If you do, you won't be there long, not in the scheme of things. That is so in any democracy.

Being separate and holding yourself above the fray also holds you above and separate from your subjects—the ones who put you there. So participate in their lives. Participate in their loves.

Participate in their pain. For it is all part of the human condition, and you are their leader. They put you there to be their leader. So do it!

They need to feel some connection with you, as they feel you are in some way an extension of them, their hopes, dreams, and expectations.

As the saying goes, "You can fool some of the people all of the time, and all of the people some of the time, but you cannot fool all of the people all of the time." In the end, people will see through the chaff and see who you really are. What will they see? And do you like it when they see the truth of you?

Your heart will shine through, should it be for good or for ill. They will know it.

Reflections

Following this interview, I looked up the word *gravitas,* as Charlemagne had used it and I thought it an unusual word. According to Merriam-Webster, *gravitas* is of Latin origin and defined as "high seriousness (as in a person's bearing or in the treatment of a subject)." I feel that this word fits the overall personality of the spirit who was Charlemagne.

I also looked up the quote at the end of the interview that begins "You can fool some of the people all of the time . . ." I was surprised to learn that, according to *Bartlett's Familiar Quotations,* it is attributed to President Abraham Lincoln. This felt equally fitting, as it came during Charlemagne's discussion about what makes a good leader.

I really liked talking with Charlemagne, but, truth be told, he made me a little nervous. I'm not sure I would want him unleashed on an unsuspecting world again. To me he still feels like an incredibly powerful medieval king. I think that if he came back and wanted to rally the troops and conquer territories, he had excellent odds of success. Although Charlemagne said that he now prefers "problem solving with words, not swords or catapults," he also said that he still sees "the honor in fighting a good, fair war." People (and spirits) are complex, so who knows which path he would take, given the chance? That's all part of the learning here on Earth. But I firmly believe that we could use more leaders who would choose nonviolent solutions.

Which brings me to Gandhi . . .

CHAPTER 8

GANDHI

Gandhi appeared to me looking as he did in his lifetime: brown skin, wire-rimmed glasses, saffron robes, and a beatific smile. His energy was positive and upbeat, but also very gentle.

Mohandas Karamchand Gandhi (more popularly known by his honorific, Mahatma Gandhi) was born on October 2, 1869, in Porbandar, India. He was most known for his philosophy of nonviolence as a way to achieve social and political progress, known as *satyagraha,* "devotion to truth." He followed these principles as a leader in the nationalist movement against British rule in India, and brought this philosophy into the popular consciousness all over the world. He was assassinated by a Hindu extremist named Nathuram Godse on January 30, 1948, in Delhi, India, at the age of 78.

When I asked Gandhi his cause of death, he said, "I was shot by a very unhappy man. I was ready to go, so I am peaceful that I went at that time. I had accomplished much of what I set out to do during that lifetime. I am still learning, and that is a very good thing."

The Interview

Susan Lander: Who was the most important person in your life, and why?

Mohandas Gandhi: God. That's where I took my marching orders. Up there *[his hands are up in prayer position]*, not down here. I was clear that I worked at the behest of God. He gave me my life, my breath, my heart and soul.

SL: How did you keep so calm and serene, even in the face of great adversity?

MG: Because there is nothing to fear. There is no reason to be fear based. Love, hate, fear, good, bad, evil? Energy, energy, energy. And belief. We have it all wrong on Earth. Everything is neutral, and there is nothing to fear.

Being on Earth is actually a great gift, for many reasons. Love it. Hope for the best if you wish. But it really does not matter. Outcome does not matter, not on a macro- or microscale. Because the soul will continue to exist, to live on, either way. You may pick up some scars, bumps, bruises, and disappointments along the way. Sometimes you will be proud of yourself for your conduct here on Earth. Sometimes you will miss the mark—slightly or by a lot. But the beautiful thing is that you always get another chance or many chances to do it better next time.

SL: You were well known for your meditation and discipline. How were you able to do this?

MG: It was not hard; it was as natural as breathing. I lived many lifetimes as a warrior, moving from violence to nonviolence. Taking the discipline of a warrior and moving it to create an army of nonviolence.

SL: I understand that you advocated extreme fasts for political and social reasons. Can you tell me more about this?

MG: It united people behind me as a force and energy for good. It gave people unified power regardless of caste or wealth. It seemed like a good idea at the moment, but now I would not advocate taking food from the mouths of those who had so little. But still it had elements of purification and oneness.

I understood that we are all equal. Certainly in the eyes of God, which is all that matters. I still believe that, more strongly than ever.

SL: Weren't you hungry during your fasts?

MG: Yes, like a tiger clawing at my stomach and innards. But I had a greater purpose, which was love. My faith carried me through, and the belief that I was doing the right thing. That was enough.

SL: Mr. Gandhi, why have you decided to talk with me and participate in this project?

MG: I am one of the originators of this project, along with Mr. Benjamin Franklin. We are at such a critical juncture in the history of mankind, and I believe that all of us in the spirit world have a unified message we would like to share. It is just the oddity of mankind and human nature, and a paradox, that famous people are often heard loud and clear. *[smiles]* It does not mean we are necessarily smarter, but we are given the gift of the bully pulpit. We feel that we would like to use this gift and ability for the greater good. Access is such a gift. It would be good if people in the public eye treated that access with the respect that it deserves.

SL: What is the message that you would like to share?

MG: Peace, love, and nonviolence. Not a cliché, but as a life choice. A choice humanity can and should make for its own survival. Its own thriving. Its own happiness.

The problem with war is that is assumes an *us* and a *them.* That is not so. That is never so. We are all related, all cousins, on both a human and a soul level.

SL: My big concern is that war seems to be humankind's default position. Do you agree? And is there a better way?

MG: Yes and yes. But there is a shift now as people are tiring of the old, time-honored ways, which they are finally seeing are of no productive use to us. Why killing for land? For food, resources, women? Even winning is not a net win in any of these cases. It may have at its essence base needs of survival, which is in some way a little more understandable. But other than that, to fight over who has the right to this land or that, this religion or that . . . no.

Winning by brute force can never bring a true victory. You can force people to obey you through brute force, but you can never change what is in their hearts. And that is why these types of victories are never permanent and need to be redone and revisited, over and over.

Capturing and enslaving humans and animals is also an abomination.

SL: So your message is . . . ?

MG: Nonviolence, nonviolence, nonviolence. Protest if you must, nothing wrong with that. There must be the means to make change in the world, to make your voices heard loudly. Indeed, we do come here to make change. But as I said, brute force does not make change. War is just a greatly magnified, aggrandized form of mass bullying. For that reason it cannot bring about true, soulful social change.

There is great power in the solidarity of the people. I do not believe that many would choose to leave their homes and families, to fight, to put themselves in danger, to risk death. I think this is just what we know. It makes us feel we are doing something. It almost seems, if the conflict is so great, how could it be solved by just talking? Or by sitting in? Or by protesting? But it can.

Harness the power of the masses, the wisdom of the masses. I do believe that people essentially have goodwill toward each other. Yes, it can be corrupted, and there can certainly be indoctrination to hate. But that is not real. That is just hating a symbol of "other," or hating the projections of their own weaknesses onto others.

But I think people just want to love and be loved. They have hearts and godly souls. War evolved as a convenient way to solve conflict over millenia. Diplomacy requires a light touch, time, effort, and goodwill. But in my mind, this is a much better way, a cheaper way, and a true and soulful way to solve conflict. I mean truly solve it at the root . . . not putting a bullying Band-Aid on the matter and imagining it solved and ended. That is untrue, unrealistic, and naïve. As well as dangerous.

I do not believe most people want to spend their time and precious lives fighting.

SL: So how do you recommend that this be changed?

MG: There must be a choice made, one that places a much greater value on solving conflict through diplomacy. Not to see it as a "gentleman's game" but as *the* way to handle conflict. People must remember, when they fight, they are fighting their brothers and sisters and cousins. Literally, sometimes, they are your blood relatives you are fighting. But whoever it is, they are always related and connected to you on an Earth and soul level. That is a fact, and it must be remembered.

You can't, you can't, you *can't* win through physical violence or emotional violence. Any kind of violence goes against all we are as souls. Somewhere in our hearts we all know this. If we didn't know it, killing and war would be easy for us. But it isn't.

War destroys both the invaders and the invaded. That is a fact. And it is well past the time that we as a society, a world, a culture, finally admit and honor that truth. And that acceptance would finally end war once and for all.

Love is everything. Love is all there is. Accept this and it will change the world. The question is, what kind of world do we want? And that, my dear friends, colleagues, loves, brothers, sisters, and cousins—that is the question. You need to be an example of the change you want to see in this world.

So this, ultimately, is your choice. Make it a good one and choose wisely.

SL: I know that you were assassinated. Do you want to talk about that?

MG: We must all pass in some way, by some method. This was just mine in that lifetime. It wasn't about me but about someone else in pain. Someone else's pain.

SL: Is there anything that you would want to say to the man who shot you?

MG: God forgive you. I forgive you. I love you. I do not choose to be victimized twice by carrying negativity, hate, and unresolved feelings toward this man.

SL: Did you think you still had unfinished business when this happened?

MG: *[smiles]* I would have "done my thing" as long as I could have. But I lived a long, good, happy life. It was not always easy, and God knows, it was often uncomfortable physically. But that was all part of my learning, my lessons. To understand, to empathize with those who were less fortunate.

My life was dedicated to my causes—to spread unconditional love and a message of unconditional peace. Without being self-aggrandizing, I came here to change the world. I believe I did. I hope I did. I am honored to be remembered. I hope it means that I did make a lasting impact toward those goals—maybe saved a life or two or ten or even a hundred—and helped give people the chance to walk their paths and be their most godly selves as well. Show them options for peace and happiness that they may not have thought of, or give them confidence when they may not have felt powerful enough to even think of creating a new reality.

It is my hope that people see this opportunity now. Organizing support—especially for the cause of nonviolence—has never been easier! I wish I had had a computer. Twitter. Can you imagine the possibilities? It boggles the mind and inflames the imagination.

SL: Are you planning to come back?

MG: No plans, at least not soon. It would take something very big. If God wishes me to go, I will, in order to serve humanity and my fellow man.

SL: What is the meaning of life?

MG: To grow and learn. And to walk your path and love as best you can. Fear not, and transcend what you think your limits are, as they are self-imposed out of fear! Even though you may have been told you couldn't do something, don't believe it. Remember that you are the holiest of holy, a beautiful, perfect, Divine being. Treat yourself that way, and treat others that way, too. If you can do that, you will earn an A-plus in the school of life, and pass to the next level!

SL: What's the next level?

MG: Your own next level of personal evolution. It is worth mentioning that the more you can do this, the more reward there is to be had! The struggle ends. Much happiness, joy, peace, and, yes, love awaits you. And you don't have to wait until you pass from this life to have it all and enjoy it. The rewards can be earned and awarded now.

SL: What were your life lessons that you came here to work on?

MG: I came here to show people a better way to live. To teach them to be more kind and loving toward each other. To show them that we are all connected, and how powerful are the possibilities arising from that.

SL: Do you feel that your campaign for nonviolent resistance was successful?

MG: To me, all that matters was that I tried. I did what I came to Earth to do. If I changed one person's perspective to value non-violence over violence, then I changed the world for the better, and for that I am grateful.

SL: Do you have any regrets?

MG: Not in the way I lived my life. I would have liked to live to be 200! And to be organizing protests and progressive change movements at this point in history. I think people are tired of war, and, thank God, many more are having spiritual awakenings. I think people finally want joy and, even more important, think that they can and should have it! The resignation people used to have is slowly becoming a remnant of the past.

SL: Was there any time when you think you got it wrong while you were here? Any position you have reconsidered?

MG: I do not think that stringent deprivation and poverty is necessary for enlightenment. It can take you to a deeper level inside yourself, where you can see things very clearly. We can also learn empathy through our own personal suffering. So it has value, and it is certainly one way of getting there. But I am not sure extremes of any sort are necessary, at least not on a consistent basis. Joyful, beautiful, and robust health can also support you in learning. I think I would explore that balance the next time. Treating yourself lovingly teaches you how to treat others lovingly as well.

SL: Can you explain that? Why is it important that you would do that?

MG: Your body is the physical extension of God. In treating yourself lovingly, you are connecting with and nurturing the Divinity within yourself. It is only through experiencing your own Divinity that you can see or understand it in others. And that teaches you how to treat others, and love them just as you love yourself.

Experiencing the Divinity in yourself is essential for your own growth. People like to bandy about the word *enlightenment,* but this is really what it means. It really is so very simple. Sometimes it is easier to see the Divinity in others, but know that you can only do that because you are Divine, too.

So what I am trying to say is that when you start to see and really feel that God or Divinity or something bigger than you is around you—and that you are somehow part of that—you are experiencing the first glimmers of enlightenment. It matters not whether these are small or large glimmers or whether you see them often. Acknowledging the web of humanity and Divinity within and around you means you are on the right track.

I urge you to see it, and if you don't come by this naturally, go looking for it! When you connect with the Divinity, you are connected with all-there-is, and everything becomes clear. Who you are, what you are, what you came to Earth to do, what your next steps are. Your seeking and searching for answers becomes an inquiry of love, peace, and expansion, not of fear and desperation. The answers are already within your grasp.

Allow your mind and heart to open. Watch the magic start to happen around you as you see possibilities that you never considered. You will see that everything you need is being drawn to you. You will have shifted your perspective from that of victim to that of seeker, and that is enough. You will have put your foot firmly on your new path, and signs and synchronicities will point you in new directions. This is the way God speaks to you, in whispers on the wind.

Review periodically your progress on your path—the new things that have happened in your life, the new way you feel as opposed to the old—and I guarantee that you will see and feel a difference.

Do not give up. Never give up. Help is on the way, and it is you.

SL: What does God mean to you?

MG: God is the life force. You can't see him but you can feel him. On one level God includes our connection to others. But to me he feels huge, and his energy and life force permeate everything. He feels like his own entity to me. Immeasurably, indescribably powerful. I feel him everywhere, and that never changes. This is how I see God.

God is a great comfort to me. I exist and float along on the cloud of this energy. It is true love. The highest, most giving, forgiving love. God sees what we do not, like a loving parent, and allows us to learn for our own benefit and for the benefit of others.

SL: Can you feel God more on the Other Side or on Earth, or is it the same?

MG: God is everywhere. It's just that people have a less conflicted view of God and reality over here. We accept this force and know it to be so, to be true, to be real.

SL: What does the word *truth* mean?

MG: There is always a little bit of interplay around the edges, because people all come to truth, or arrive at truth, from their own perspectives. But there are certain spiritual truths or tenets, like "love your neighbor as yourself."

SL: And if you don't follow these spiritual truths?

MG: If you don't follow them, you will be violating spiritual laws, such as "do no harm." Or you will run the risk of violating another person's autonomy. That is the one that gives us all the most difficulty. You can never really control another in any way, except by coercion.

SL: Do you have any advice you would like to offer to our world's leaders?

MG: Please work together and change the world! Do you realize you have the individual ability to directly improve the lives of everybody on the planet? It is a huge, great, golden gift. Truly a spectacular opportunity of immense value. This is what you came here to do. Don't waste it. This is not a dress rehearsal.

Remember, power is not the end, but the means for great social change and the evolution and advancement of mankind.

SL: Did you have a guru?

MG: Yes, I had a teacher. We are all each other's teachers, though. To me he was a spiritual advisor, nothing more. We all need spiritual teachers if we are to seek spiritual truth. It is their job! To think about these things and share what they know.

To me he was not God. I did not give away my power to him. But I did ask him questions, receive answers. There is nothing wrong with asking for and receiving help and answers from those who know more in a particular area or arena. His specialty was spiritual matters. He was a man of God—I knew that then, and I know him now. He is special and unique in his understanding of spiritual matters. Better, he understands both people and God. What makes them work, what motivates them. Why people might do the things they do. Why people are drawn to certain situations. Why they act in certain ways.

People just want to be loved, accepted, needed, and understood at their core, at their essence. The way they act stems from that, even though it may not always seem that way.

I think that people are beautiful and fascinating. Endlessly interesting. Lack of awareness of ourselves can lead us into trouble in many ways, though. Blind faith, unquestioning, is very dangerous, because it leads people to act without a moral center.

Power can be used for good or for ill by those who wield it. It is a great and grave responsibility when others place their moral compass upon you. You must act with responsibility and discernment. Otherwise it is not healthy; it is ego based and must be discouraged.

For those who place their moral compass on others, relying on others instead of what is within them, here is my advice: You are perfect. You are Divine and holy. You must follow your own guidance, what is in your heart. It is a good thing to seek answers to your questions. It is a good thing to have questions at all! But you are unique, we all are, and no one person knows the answers to all of your questions except you and God. So seek counsel, and then make your own decisions.

If someone wants to make your decisions for you, run the other way! They are not coming from God, their answers are not coming from God, they are acting from their own ego-selves. And that is unacceptable. You do not need them. Take what you need from teachers here and there. If you have a good teacher, by all means keep him or her in your life as an added value. But it is never a good idea to hand a person your autonomy and power.

SL: What kind of questions did you ask your teacher?

MG: Questions about how to handle situations with others, relationships. Sometimes bigger decisions like campaigns—was x or y an appropriate thing to do in the spiritual scheme of things.

SL: What does "the spiritual scheme of things" mean?

MG: Was it on my path spiritually as well as others'? Was whatever I was considering keeping within the basic spiritual rules—was it loving to myself and my fellow man, and truly respecting of our spiritual and godly natures? I did not want to infringe on others due to my own agenda.

I also liked to talk with him about what might happen after I left the earth.

SL: Is the Other Side what you thought?

MG: The love is what I thought. The feeling. I had intellectual and heart hope that it would feel this way, although it is truly indescribable. Gentle, peaceful, a continual warm embrace. Can you imagine a place where you are truly your best self all the time? And that is here, where I am now. It is why people seek to know it, and to know God.

I think on some level we seek that feeling and try to find it on Earth. We work toward that. But the problem is that we are so disconnected from it on Earth, and there is so much negativity, poverty, need, pain, crime, and disrespect that it is so hard to find. But this energy of God is everywhere. You can take your blinders off and see it, feel it.

SL: Why do you think people are drawn to gurus?

MG: Because they are looking for self-acceptance, but think they can find it through acceptance by others and through belonging to something greater than themselves. But beware, you can never find salvation through other people. That must come from within, and is easily accessible through your relationship with yourself and with God. The acceptance and love is innate; just grasp it. Hold out your hands and know that they are already filled.

Please don't misunderstand me—spiritual teachers are very valuable and necessary! They have additional knowledge and perspective to share, because again, it is their preferred area of study and it is their job to share it. All I am saying is please keep it in perspective. They are no better or worse than you. They may even make destructive choices. Their job and their perspective as a spiritual teacher is just different and may be useful.

However, people place additional emotional value on the teachings of gurus, and they perceive the person as more elevated or worthy. As we are all part of the same Divine force, no one person is more worthy than another. People may consider others unworthy for class or caste reasons, but this is just the ego-mind looking to place elevated value on themselves. And that is always illusory by definition.

SL: Do people come to Earth to be gurus? If so, what is the lesson?

MG: Yes, people definitely come here to be spiritual teachers. How they actualize that varies greatly. It is a complex lesson and can be difficult, as life lessons are. As a spiritual teacher, you are really the bridge between the self and God, both individually and in a broader sense. The ego and issues of power and abuse of spiritual authority must often be addressed.

SL: Did people think of you as a guru?

MG: Yes, definitely. They did like to talk to me, follow me. I tried to never abuse that, and to keep my higher ideals in mind.

SL: What were your higher ideals?

MG: That people could understand our essential sameness, and our worthiness to receive love and grace. That everyone deserves love, grace, and respect. It was important to bring everyone to the same level. I was drawn, driven, to help impart that lesson. I think I did that. I hope I did that.

SL: What does the word *grace* mean to you?

MG: That people allow the grace of God to touch them. The love and gifts are all around them—already bestowed upon them or waiting to be bestowed upon them—if they could only see it.

SL: Are there benefits to being a spiritual teacher?

MG: Oh yes! Of course! It is an excellent and worthy path for learning. As people ask questions, the teacher can become enlightened along with the student. It can be an exciting process for all who are involved. You sometimes exchange roles of teacher and student. It is very enlightening and stimulating if approached in the right way, as an open-minded exploration. And fun, too.

SL: Any final thoughts?

MG: Just love yourself and others. See yourself as unique and special, as we all are! Find your gifts and share them. That is why you're here.

SL: Thank you so much for your time and thought and love in your answers. It is such an honor, and you have given us much to think about.

MG: Thank you. May many blessings be bestowed upon all of you, and may you see clearly the blessings that you already have.

Reflections

Connecting with Gandhi was such a spiritually uplifting experience. And though he is very wise and very much a teacher, I also found him surprisingly practical, down-to-earth, cheerful, and endearing.

After the interview, I realized that one of his statements, "You need to be an example of the change you want to see in this world," sounded familiar. After some Internet research, I learned that this was close to something Gandhi wrote: "We but mirror the world. All the tendencies present in the outer world are to be found in the world of our body. If we could change ourselves, the tendencies in the world would also change."

As to the identity of Gandhi's guru, it is possible that he is referring to Gopal Krishna Gokhale. In Gandhi's autobiography, *The Story of My Experiments with Truth,* he calls Gokhale his mentor and guide.

My next visit was from Albert Einstein, who offers a very different type of wisdom, and bridges the gap between spirituality and science.

CHAPTER 9

ALBERT EINSTEIN

When Albert Einstein appeared, he filled my field of vision with equations, starting with his most famous, from his theory of special relativity: $E = mc^2$. Then I saw him holding a wooden pointer and standing in front of a blackboard that had formulas written in white chalk. (Creating a classroom scene like this is unusual for a spirit to do, but given the difficult subject matter we were about to discuss, I thought later that it was really smart of him to turn it into a fun little story.) He had wild, shoulder-length white hair and a bushy white mustache, and he was wearing a brown suit with wide-set white pinstripes. Although I normally hear spirits speaking in modern English regardless of when and where they lived, when he spoke, it sounded to me like English with a German accent.

Albert Einstein was born on March 14, 1879, in Ulm, Württemberg, Germany. He was a Nobel Prize–winning physicist who revolutionized science and transformed the way we look at space, time, gravity, matter, and energy. He is most famous for formulating the theory of special relativity and the equation $E = mc^2$, which expresses that mass and energy are the same physical entity and can be changed into each other. Einstein's groundbreaking theories also helped usher in the nuclear age. He died of a ruptured aortic aneurysm on April 18, 1955, in Princeton, New Jersey, at the age of 76. According to him, "We must all go sometime and die of something. I led a good life, and I left a good legacy."

The Interview

Susan Lander: Hello, Mr. Einstein.

Albert Einstein: Hello, Miss Lander.

SL: Thank you for coming to talk with me! What are you working on right now on the Other Side?

AE: I am working on many engineering projects, including advanced, safe, and stable nuclear fission and fusion, and how to bring time travel into the mainstream on Earth and other planets. This knowledge could be transmitted to scientists on Earth, but as a society you are not quite ready for this. It is just not time yet. But it will be eventually.

For now I would like to give you a little lesson. I would like to start teaching you how to understand and manipulate time.

SL: Okay, then! How can we understand the nature of time?

AE: Time is malleable; time is mutable. Time is what you make it. Do you understand? It is never what you think it is . . . rather, it is *exactly* what you think it is.

SL: Sounds like a paradox to me.

AE: It is.

[He smiles, then shows me an image of a galaxy expanding and contracting.]

Time is infinite. It expands, it contracts—just like the rest of the universe. Let it.

What if you could go anywhere, do anything, be unlimited? That is the nature of time. It is unlimited, because it is never an absolute. It is like a glass of water. You can add some, drain some, and then add some more whenever you choose.

You really can buy time! Think of it as a limitless commodity for you to partake of. Plus, it's free. But, like your computer, it does have some absolute rules, like an operating system. If you understand the system and learn the code, you can make it work for you.

In order for you to master this new skill of understanding and manipulating time, first you must let go of your idea of yourself as a finite being. Thinking of yourself as limited will keep you from mastering this new skill.

[I am suddenly feeling like the Neo character in the movie The Matrix. *How can you believe, or know, that you can do something that seems impossible?]*

SL: I understand what you are saying, but how do you get to that knowing?

AE: All time originates with you. Many people will be happy to know that they really are the center of their universe, and everything does spin in orbit around them! *[smiles]*

SL: Can you go into the past?

AE: Yes.

SL: The future?

AE: Yes. But there are multiple futures, existing concurrently on different planes of existence, different trajectories.

SL: How about the past?

AE: Same. But that's only in the paradigm of linear time. You're asking, *Who am I, and where do I exist in relation to everything else?* You are only thinking in the limited notion of one timeline, the current timeline, as you understand it.

You must understand that this is not true. Let go of these preconceived, limited notions of what you can and cannot do. Understand that we are all capable of so much more. If you only knew!

I would say that we are all magical beings, as we have the unlimited capacity to create our realities in an alchemical fashion. But, on the other hand, it is just physics, which at its heart is the finite code and the set rules of the functioning of the universe.

SL: So you're saying: just learn the code and you have it. What is the code?

AE: You don't have to learn the particulars, but it helps to give you a framework. Just start by knowing that time, like everything else—including the building blocks of the universe—expands and contracts. Then you can start to adjust to the notion that you can move within that, be the center of the universe, and have it revolve around you.

Try this experiment: Picture yourself unhooking from the nature of time, from your current time stream. Say to yourself, "I am not in time, I am not in time, I am just me. I am the center of my universe, and everything else is in orbit around me." Feel how everything else fades into the background. You will feel very centered and powerful. For the moment, you have separated from the dimension of time, from the feeling of time. You see, you don't really need it. People are so concerned with being on time and staying on time, but that is a fallacy.

It is no different than using a ruler. Use time when you want to, otherwise put it in a drawer and close it. Time is everyone's security blanket. It makes people feel solid on Earth. But the truth is, it's just another thing—with a spirit and a grand use—but a thing you can think of as an inanimate object, and a thing you can manipulate at will . . . with apologies to the atoms, electrons, and quarks that are spinning within it. But that is another story. They are just the building blocks of all that is around us. They are no more alive or dead than that table. It is just a matter of your perspective.

You have choices. You do not have to give time that grand power that we on Earth give it. Start to function outside it and it will become a habit. Use time only when you need it. It does not need to become your lord and master, the be-all and end-all, how you mark the passage of your life. Start to separate from that. You are so much bigger than this, more talented than this, to be stuck in a limited notion of the framework we live and function in. Don't buy it. Be curious, be the magician, wave your magic wand, and experiment. Start by covering up the clocks. I know this will make many people uneasy. But just think, *I am so much bigger than this. I don't need a big ruler to run my life. A ruler is just a tool to use when we need to make something fit in a limited space. And unless that is the case in the moment, I don't have to. I choose not to.*

Time gives us a feeling of stability, order, and certainty. And in the relative chaos that is Earth, people feel they need that. But time should revolve around you, not the other way around. It is so limiting. You are cutting off your natural ability to transcend time. Living within time is a habit; you can unlearn it. It is merely a shift in perspective. It starts that way, so *start*. Resolve to never be a slave to time anymore. It does not own you. Accept that and rejoice in it, and it will free you in so many ways.

SL: So the mantra is, *Time is like a ruler: I will put it in a drawer and close it when I don't need it or want it.*

AE: Yes, exactly. And never forget: It's a tool, it's a watch, it's a grand treadmill or conveyor belt. Step on it and off it at will.

I have given you the first key. It is up to each of you to start using it. I can't do that for you.

We must seek to find solidity within ourselves, not externally. That is the old paradigm, before we knew other ways to exist. I think that each of you will find it extremely liberating.

Well, I enjoyed teaching this little lesson about time. Thank you for the opportunity to come through, and to be up here in front of a class of eager students once again.

SL: Thank you so much.

Reflections

This was a challenging interview for me as a medium. When spirits communicate, they have only a medium's frame of reference to work with—in other words, they are limited to the dictionaries in our heads. I am not an expert in physics (far from it!), so Einstein did the best he could with who and what he had to work with. I think that these concepts are just difficult for most human brains to comprehend; it wouldn't have mattered *who* was trying to talk to me about it. But he did have a sense of humor about it all, and was able to creatively supplement his words with images to help me understand the concepts. Despite the challenges, I think it worked well, and I enjoyed my lesson in time with Albert Einstein.

My next visitor, Henry Ford, lived during the same era as Albert Einstein. Thankfully, he did not want to talk about physics. As one might expect, he wanted to talk about cars and money.

CHAPTER 10

HENRY FORD

While I was trying to work on my budget, wondering who might give me good financial advice, Henry Ford popped in. He was already on my list of people who I thought would participate in this project, but I had no idea what he'd want to talk about—I assumed he'd just want to talk about cars! He was wearing a charcoal-gray suit, and his energy felt very strong, fiercely smart, and focused. He kind of "barked" his advice at me. I could feel that he was very tough but with an unexpectedly soft side.

Henry Ford was born into a family of farmers on July 30, 1863, in Wayne County, Michigan. He left home at 16 and went on to become an enormously successful businessman, industrialist, and founder of the Ford Motor Company. The innovations he pioneered, such as the development of the assembly line, which revolutionized mass production, and the concept of paying workers a living wage, changed the structure of society. His technological advances and creation of the Model T car made the automobile an affordable necessity rather than a luxury item. He was the force behind an industry whose impact includes moving the U.S. from the agricultural to industrial era. He died of a cerebral hemorrhage on April 7, 1947, in Dearborn, Michigan, at the age of 83. Of that, he said to me, "At least it was fast."

The Interview

Susan Lander: You were enormously financially successful. What advice can you give to people who are seeking financial abundance?

Henry Ford: The problem is, most people have their money in a tight little box. Open it up and let it breathe! Hold your hands out and let them be filled, overflowing, with money flowing all around them. Love your money and it will love you.

Let it be unlimited like your heart, like your love. Expand it until it's like the sky. Envision it becoming a huge money box, jostling for room in your life because it's so crowded. How big will you let it grow?

Two pieces of advice: First, it's okay to go to where the money is. And second, your favorite money will be that which you give away to good causes.

SL: So if I had to sum up the advice on financial success from you and Andy Warhol, it would be: Be real, come from the same place love comes from, and go where the money is.

HF: The connection between money and love is an important one. It's a universal law, and it's where so many people go wrong these days. Money without love, money without heart, is out of context somehow. It's disconnected from who we are. That's why people who make money with just an ego motivation seem so disconnected, and everyone knows it.

True happiness can never come this way, although it can be fun for a while! It's like bathing in a sea of the merest fluff. It lacks the natural sustenance that comes from that heart energy. I think that this is why people who make, accrue, and acquire money this way are so afraid their money is going to up and disappear. It lacks the substantial and well-rounded quality of the wealth held by the heart-based folks.

SL: I keep thinking of Steve Jobs. He had such integrity somehow.

HF: Exactly. Everyone wanted a piece of his wealth, and just about everyone has their own piece of it—a tangible representation of it that they can hold in their hands. How brilliant!

The same was true for my cars! It was about more than just owning a car. I knew what I was going for. Give the people jobs. Make money. Give back. An endless cycle of wealth, flowing outward like a spiral, originating from the eye of the hurricane . . . me. [smiles]

Always know what you are going for in all the things you do. It will help move the energy and bring about the results you desire.

SL: The Apple logo even looks sort of like a heart. All curvy and female and voluptuous.

HF: Adam and Eve and the Garden of Eden. Original sin? I don't think so. Original beauty. The Apple logo was so inspired.

SL: There are two areas of controversy that I want to ask you about. First, I understand that you didn't like unions, and that there were several years of difficult and even violent incidents leading up to the unionization at the Ford Motor plant.

Second, I read that there were allegations that you were anti-Semitic due to some particular associations. Specifically, *The Dearborn Independent* newspaper, which was owned by you, published a series of negative articles about Jewish people from 1920 to 1927. I understand that you later published a retraction and sold the paper. In addition, I read that you accepted a medal from the Third Reich and continued to do business with the Nazi regime in Germany. Do you want to comment?

HF: I was still a product of the times, my dear, a product of the times. We are all influenced to some degree by what goes on around us. But I also had strongly held convictions at the time and acted in accordance with them, so I feel completely comfortable with that now. Power can corrupt faster than the blink of an eye. I believe people must have eternal vigilance and a strong moral center to guard against the effects of that.

My motto: always listen to people and what they have to say. It puts your finger on the pulse of the moment, and you might learn something. And while you're listening, please do not be hardheaded or stubborn in your beliefs. It's important for your growth. I wish I had been a little more open-minded. You can never be open-minded enough.

And everyone wants to be understood and heard, so give them their time. You don't have to agree or disagree. It's just a matter of basic human respect.

With regard to your original question about what happened with the union, I didn't like unions because I believed they didn't always have the workers' best interests at heart. But for the record, I do not condone violence in any way, and I never did. I am sorry that things got out of hand at one or two times during my lifetime, and for that I did and do ask forgiveness. Souls have the opportunity to learn and grow and to see more clearly, no matter which side we are on.

With regard to the question about Hitler and the allegations of anti-Semitism, it is so easy to pigeonhole people, but, my dear, we are all so complex. Sometimes we make mistakes. Sometimes in trying not to judge, we become complicit.

SL: What do you mean?

HF: Sometimes it might be better to avoid the appearance of cooperation, either in the interest of self-preservation or to support your own ideals. But I know this about me—it's just not in my soul to hate. Ultimately, when it comes right down to it, I only have to answer to myself. I don't feel any need to defend myself at this point for any actions or inactions I took while I was on Earth. I stuck to my ideals and my philosophy the best I could, and I left the earth a better place than when I arrived.

I made my mark on history, evolution, and society. I improved technology. And the cars . . . oh, the cars. How I loved them! My Model T Ford, my signature car, was my labor of love. How to best get from point A to point B fascinated me. I knew instinctively that it was a quality-of-life issue. We all had to use cars on Earth, so I wanted to make it the best experience possible. I think when it came right down to it, I wanted to make everybody happy, and this was one way to do it. It made me happy, too. It was my gift to humanity, and I am still so proud of my contribution.

Forgive me if I don't want to talk more about Hitler and anti-Semitism. I would rather focus on joy and good things. I like to believe that my life and my soul are much more about that. I'll just ask people to avoid snap judgments. They weren't there, and it is impossible for anyone to know how they would act in a particular situation. Walk a mile in my shoes, as they say, and then judge if you must. But I would prefer that you don't. At any rate, it's out of my hands at this point.

SL: You said you stuck to your ideals and philosophy. What were they?

HF: To listen and not judge. To not condemn people unless they have wronged you personally. Even then, try to understand their perspective. It doesn't mean you have to like it. But you might learn something, and at least you will understand where they're coming from. This will help depersonalize the situation and give you breathing room to respond in a measured, appropriate way. From this perspective you can see much more clearly, make better decisions and better choices, and have better relationships.

SL: Do you have any regrets? Do you wish you had done anything differently?

HF: Like I said, I want to focus on where I went right, instead of where I missed the mark. I like to focus on the good instead of the evil. That is my right, and I am going to take it and exercise that right. A point of personal privilege, if you will.

SL: What life lessons did you come here to work on?

HF: I came here to develop and invent technology, and move technology forward, for the betterment of humanity. I really wanted to help people and to make their lives better. I think I did that, and I accomplished most of what I came here to do. When I got to the Other Side and looked back at my life, I was satisfied. I wasn't perfect, of course, and had much room for improvement. I wish I had more balance in my life and made more time for my family. Maybe I'll have better luck with that next time.

SL: What do you do on the Other Side?

HF: My job is to work with people who have just come back from Earth, to get them reacclimated to being here. It's like I'm a tour guide. It's fun for me, to see their eyes light up as they reimagine and remember the possibilities of being limitless beings. All that potential! It's easy to forget that when you're in the confines of a body on Earth or wherever you're returning from. There is no place like going Home. It is truly paradise here. It is where hate ends and possibilities begin.

SL: Do you have a soul mate there?

HF: Yes.

SL: Do you live with her?

HF: Most of the time. Is there a point to this?

SL: The point is, are you happy and fulfilled now? Are you with someone you love?

HF: The answer is yes. On both counts.

SL: Are you planning to come back to Earth?

HF: Not right now. I'm enjoying my life here and spending my time with people I love. My wife is here. Edsel is here. *[Edsel was the only son of Henry and his wife, Clara.]* My friends are here. I have no need to go rushing back to Earth. Why would I? Earth is a very tough place.

SL: What is the one thing you think people misunderstood when it comes to you and your place in history?

HF: That I'm not so calculating. I like things the way I like them, and I'm good at getting things done. But I don't think I'm quite as hard-nosed as people made me out to be. I had a vision, I generally wanted to do the right thing by everybody, and I got pretty close. Overall, I feel I was successful at the game of life.

I wish you all luck and as much success as I had. Just follow your heart, follow your vision, and remain steadfast. Put one step in front of the other, and I think you'll get pretty close to achieving your dreams.

SL: A final question about history, if you please. I just looked up some of your quotes on the Internet, and I was very interested in these: "I don't read history. That's in the past. I'm thinking of the future," and "History is more or less bunk." Can you talk some more about this topic? Do you still feel the same way?

HF: History serves only as a useful guideline for helping you make better choices the next time. There is no time except "now." I understood it to some degree then, but now I *really* understand it. As it turns out, I was right about that concept! Money is a good example. You can't take money with you. All you have is what exists in the moment.

You can't change history, at least your own history. You can only learn from it, at best, and make better choices. That, I believe, is our responsibility as productive citizens of the world, or of the universe! You can at least try. You owe yourself that, as well as others. We are all connected.

SL: Thank you very much. Do you have any advice you would like to give leaders who are in power now?

HF: Just listen to the people . . . just listen to the people! They are smart. They know what they want, or at least what they need. Understand what is essential to people.

Know that they can take you out and cut you off in a matter of minutes. Know you are not infallible. That's a big danger that comes with power. A swelled head is very unattractive, and people can see it a mile away. It separates you from people. Once that happens, you're functioning on your own and people know it.

You are a representative of the people. They put you there; they put their faith and fate and trust in you. That deserves the utmost respect and care. Give that to them. If you don't do that, you are on your own, and that is a very lonely place. It will stifle your creativity and power, too. You draw your power from the people, and they can take it away. Don't forget that. Don't abuse their faith and trust in you.

SL: What would you do if you were President of the United States right now?

HF: I would clean things up. Clean house. If the people who worked for me wouldn't get with my program, they would be swept out with the garbage. Where is the integrity these days? That's what I want to know. I would insist on having people with integrity around me.

SL: What would your "program" be?

HF: Integrity at all costs. I don't suffer fools gladly.

SL: What would be your definition of a fool?

HF: The ones who don't have a moral center, who can be easily swayed and are just wishy-washy. I may not be saying this artfully, but what I'm trying to say is: Say what you mean, mean what you say, and then stand up for that. Put some backbone behind it. But this endless spin machine? Kowtowing, toadying, sucking up to those in the pursuit of endless power and endless cash, and the eroding loss of integrity that comes with that? That would end under my watch. The buck stops with the one on top. Maybe I am hard-line, but I just wouldn't tolerate that type of dynamic and manipulation. Unfortunately, that is the current dynamic in fashion among the power elite.

There is a better way. Governing from integrity does work. So people can agree or disagree with you, but everyone respects a moral center. On a very basic level we all want to be treated that way.

I believe the current President, Barack Obama, does have a strong moral center. He knows who he is, what he wants, and where he's going. My advice to President Obama: You may feel the odds are stacked against you, but keep operating from a place of integrity. If you feel something is wrong, just say no. You are in charge, and you do not have to do it. That is always your right regardless of the role you are playing at the moment.

SL: Like theater?

HF: Yes. *[smiles]* There is something of theater to it. But you can break the culture, at least in your own small way. Stick to your ideals and never waver, particularly not in service to those who believe in gains at all costs. I think he is a good man. I think we would be good friends if I were still there.

SL: Why do you say that?

HF: I like him. I admire him. I would not want his job, not right now. Maybe later. On the other hand, maybe it would just be the ultimate challenge to turn this thing around. Agree with him or not—and I would agree with him in more ways than not—that is the mark of a great leader. While I appreciate his conciliatory nature and being a man of the people, I think he can be more steadfast when it comes to action. He is President—here's his chance. He gets to do this right now.

That said, he has taken on an immense responsibility, being in this position at this time in our human evolution and our country's history. He deserves respect and admiration. It is the hardest job in the world at this time, and I admire and respect him for taking it on and seeing it through.

SL: What about filibusters, blocking votes, and the system dynamic right now in Washington?

HF: I do not agree with it, but I do not think that this is insurmountable. However, my advice is to operate from integrity, never compromise your values, and do your part as best you can.

SL: I have a few short questions about cars. What do you think about a person's "need for speed"? Do you think it's related to impatience or something else?

HF: People's cars are an extension of themselves. The way they handle their cars is analogous to how they handle themselves in the world. Are they smooth? Are they jerky? Are they impatient? Do they like to take risks or not? All of these personality types can be seen and reflected in a person's driving habits and in their choice of cars.

People's cars are reflections of themselves in many ways—who they are and who they want to be. Look at, for example, a red sports car. Is the person daring, or do they just want to be? Either is okay; it's just a reflection of themselves.

SL: What do you think of all-electric cars and hybrid cars that have both a gasoline engine and an electric motor?

HF: I wish I had invented them. I did think of them, but at the time we were very far from even imagining them into reality.

SL: If you were here right now, what kind of car would you drive?

HF: A sport-utility vehicle, an SUV. It would make me look sportier than I am *[smiles]*, but it's very utilitarian, like me.

SL: Were you an aggressive driver?

HF: No, because I was aware of the potential harm that could come from reckless driving. I did not want to harm anyone—me or someone else.

SL: Would you buy a car from another country?

HF: Now I would. The world is a very small place. Globalization made it so. There is very little difference between a car made here or overseas, but that was not always the case. Of course I can be nationalistic, but in my present location I am not inclined to be so.

SL: What is one thing people could appreciate more about being on Earth?

HF: The enormous potential for doing good, for making people's lives better. Earth is nothing more than a huge alchemical machine. We can all be alchemical wizards and make our dreams happen.
Staying small is not where it's at! Grow. Prosper. Explore your potential. Never accept limits. If you feel a limitation, it's your own.

SL: The part of me that feels that certain groups of people don't have equal opportunities is objecting to that statement.

HF: I'm not saying that people won't experience obstacles to their growth or success. Indeed, that is all part of the Earth experience. But don't let the bastards get you down! Ride roughshod over them if you must. But I'm saying, do everything you can to reach your personal limits, and then keep going and growing some more. You never know what is waiting for you on the other side of your own perceived limitations. You may love it! Allow yourself to be surprised. And just know that you came here to explore the depth and breadth of your greatest potential. Transcend your own outer limits and you can leave here proud of what you've accomplished. Don't we all want that? At least I did—that was for sure.

SL: So why did you choose to participate in this project?

HF: Because I feel I have an unusual perspective to share, both from what I learned on Earth and what I now know on the Other Side. It is indeed a gift to have this broader perspective. Live and learn, and I hope I have. I am happy to share a bit of the Divine Other Side and the afterlife with the folks at home.

Best of luck to all of you. Always have faith in yourself. And most of all, never give a moment's thought to what you think you can't do. The sky's the limit, and you really can have it all.

Wishing you lots of luck, love, heart, and money—in that order.

This is Henry Ford, signing off from the spirit world. End transmission.

Reflections

I found Henry Ford's perspective on the importance of the heart connection with money to be very interesting. It does seem to present an opportunity to become more abundant financially.

During my Internet research, I was fascinated by many of Henry Ford's quotations. If you'd like to learn more, a good resource is the Benson Ford Research Center's site at: www.thehenryford.org/research/henryFordQuotes.aspx. I was surprised to read his quotes in which he viewed history as "bunk" and unimportant except as a chance to do something differently. However, I think this is a great perspective; so many of us get stuck in our past, haunted by what might have been.

"Haunted by one's past" would be an apt description of the next participant in this book, World War II filmmaker and photographer Leni Riefenstahl. She is most famous (or infamous) for her film about the Nazi Party, *Triumph of the Will,* and her association with Adolf Hitler.

_____

CHAPTER 11

LENI RIEFENSTAHL

This was the most difficult piece for me to write, due to my own Jewish heritage and to Leni Riefenstahl's indelible connection to Hitler. I spent most of my life avoiding Holocaust literature and film. In connecting with the German filmmaker, not only did I have to look at it, I had to viscerally *feel* it from the perspective of one who lived through it and feels personally responsible for swaying people's opinions in support of Adolf Hitler. It brought me back in time to a place I never wanted to be.

Leni Riefenstahl was born Berta Helene Amalie Riefenstahl on August 22, 1902, in Berlin, Germany. She was a director, producer, actor, photographer, painter, and dancer. Although her innovative filmmaking techniques receive critical acclaim to this day, she is most known for her personal association with Adolf Hitler. In the 1930s, with the support of the Nazi Party, she directed documentary films that touted Aryan superiority and showcased the power and unity of the Nazis to the world. These films include *Victory of the Faith (Sieg des Glaubens)*, which was commissioned by Hitler, and *Triumph of the Will (Triumph des Willens)*, her most infamous film, a documentary of the 1934 Nazi Party convention in Nuremberg. It remains widely regarded as pro-Nazi propaganda, although she protested this interpretation.

She was detained by Allied forces after World War II. Although she was officially cleared of complicity with war crimes, her career as a filmmaker was essentially over. After completing the film she had been working on, *Lowland (Tiefland),* she shifted to a career in photography. Then, just before she turned 100, she released her final documentary, *Impressions Under Water (Impressionen unter Wasser).* She died of lung cancer the next year, on September 8, 2003, in Pöcking, Germany, at the age of 101. According to her, her cause of death was: "Extreme old age . . . and a problem with my lungs. I was like a cat with nine lives. At least, it felt that way sometimes!"

Over her lifetime, she continued to have extremely conflicted feelings about her association with Hitler and the Nazi Party. This was evident in an interview she gave for the 1993 documentary *The Wonderful, Horrible Life of Leni Riefenstahl (Die Macht der Bilder: Leni Riefenstahl,* or *The Power of the Image: Leni Riefenstahl),* and I most definitely noticed similar emotions during our interview.

In our interview, Leni talked about her feelings about her role in history. She delivered a strong statement about what happens when people get swept away on a wave of nationalism during difficult times, and the need for personal responsibility for the collective—a message that is woven through all of the preceding interviews in this book like a tapestry.

The interview took a rather unexpected turn when she asked for forgiveness from God and said that she has to live with herself and what she did. I could feel that this was very painful and challenging for her, but she was really determined to do it. After all, she has passed. Nobody was forcing her to revisit her actions, but she did it anyway, which I found quite remarkable. At the end of the interview, she issued a warning that we must remain vigilant against the threat of genocide, and stated that she came through to try to prevent similar situations—this, I believe, is part of her personal penance.

The Interview

Susan Lander: You lived to be over 100. What is your secret of such longevity?

Leni Riefenstahl: I am a survivor. That is my essence.

SL: The Hitler documentary . . .

LR: History needs documenters of history.

Please suspend your judgment and listen to my story. I want to be heard and seen for who I am. That's what all of us want, isn't it? But in that lifetime I told my story and my thoughts through the camera. I do not care that I challenge you. Indeed, I know that I do. Controversy is my helpmate; it gets my work noticed. Then you can draw your own conclusions. My job is to give you the information to make informed judgments.

I try to be impassive in presenting my material—that is my job. Isn't it funny how you can see something factual and neutral, and assign it emotional meaning? On one level it's just a happening, a fact. But then you put it together with what you know or think you know, and it takes on a new meaning. In my case, people didn't like the subject, so they connected me—the impassive photographer, director, and documenter—and I became part of their emotional reactions. Not fair, although I can't say I'm surprised. People's emotional natures are part of their beauty. Why do you think I loved photographing them? But I do have a heart, I do love, and I do feel. I am no different from you. And I want to be remembered for that.

If I photographed something known to be cruel, it does not mean that I am cruel. It means I was merely a photographer photographing something cruel.

I just wanted to show the truth in all I did, as close as one could come to it. I'm not perfect, maybe I failed sometimes at that, but God knows I tried to show it—the truth, in all its mutability, fallibility, inconsistency, and beauty. The truth, in all its simplicity, complexity, ambiguity. People want the truth to be so simple. It is not. It is rarely as we see it or believe it. A mother's love, maybe, is the truest thing. Beyond that, all is up for grabs. Put that in your pipe and smoke it.

SL: Why did you want to do this interview, and why now?

LR: I want to clear my name.

SL: What do you want people to remember from reading this interview?

LR: That I am not evil.

SL: Do you think your film about Hitler made a difference? If so, how?

LR: I don't know. I was just swept away on the wave of nationalism that all of us in Germany were affected by at that time. We were all looking for a savior in the wrong places. We were scared, and fear has a way of removing inhibitions. Did we know all wasn't right? Yes. Somewhere in our hearts we knew. But how many of us turned our faces and wanted to believe that things would get better? At least we hoped that they would. The capacity of people to look the other way and pretend that things are different, the way we want them to be, is enormous.

I did not know the full extent of Hitler's evil at the time. No one on the outside really did. He was amoral, sadistic, and cruel beyond the capacity of the human psyche to comprehend. To do what he did—to preside over what he led—defies logic, reason, and the understanding of any feeling person.

Do I feel responsible for rallying people to his support at the time? Yes, I do, and may God forgive me for that. I was swept up in it. It was morally reprehensible, although I didn't see it that way. I didn't want to see. I just hope that history ultimately looks upon me kindly. I was no different from scores of people in a nation that truly wanted to believe that their future was far brighter than the present that they were living.

Now I hope you better understand how this could happen. I do feel misunderstood fundamentally, and I hope that you all find it in your hearts to forgive me for the pain I have caused. I am not evil. I just participated, perhaps unknowingly and unwittingly, in an unspeakable chapter in history. I would rather leave it in the past; for me, that is so. But it is my hope that people hold in their minds that this blind nationalism, and national fervor to the exclusion of all reason, could easily happen again. Just look around. All is not black-and-white. Perhaps we all share the capacity to be somewhere in between. So choose wisely.

SL: What happened after you passed and went to the Other Side?

LR: I went through a life review, as we all do after we pass. We consider our lives, our choices, and what we would have done differently. We put that lifetime to rest in order for us to continue moving forward.

SL: If you had a chance to do it again, would you still have made the same choices?

LR: I like to believe not, to the extent that I contributed to further mayhem. But it is hard to know for sure. People are multifaceted. We do make mistakes, some more grave than others. Please do not hold me responsible for all of the things that happened during that time period. My responsibility is only for my piece of that grand puzzle. But I have to live with myself permanently, and to know the truth about that period in history and my role in it.

Now it is your turn to hold yourselves accountable for what is happening now. This is why I decided to come through. Not to be put on trial, but to clear my name to the extent that I can, and to talk with you about personal responsibility. If you see something happening that is morally reprehensible, and you stand by and let it be, are you any better than I was then? Are you taking full responsibility for how you are living your life? What about your personal responsibility to society and to humanity? Look within to answer these questions. Then if you still want to judge me for the role I played in history, so be it. I will have done what I came here to do.

None of us are perfect during our lifetimes. It's that continuum, you know? Where you are at any given time, between who you are and who you want to be.

So am I guilty as charged? Should I be in a permanent state of penance for my actions? Should there be universal retribution? That is not for you to say. Ultimately, that is between God and me. And I will always have to live with myself.

SL: Why do you think people supported Hitler and his vision?

LR: They were united behind him in his vision of the Nazi Germany and the Third Reich. He was able to exploit people's need to belong to something greater than themselves, and to unite them in that vision. That was why he was so powerful and so dangerous. That type of power is so fraught with danger in the hands of the wrong leader. If for good, it's magical. If not, well, you know . . .

SL: You mentioned God earlier. What is your relationship with God?

LR: That is the whole interview. God is everyone. God is everywhere. *God* is a catchall term for humanity, the universe, all we are, all we could be. Our responsibility to ourselves, nature, and others.

God is the force that powers the universe. It is steadfast. It has rules such as "karma." Essentially, karma is the force or consequences generated by your actions, and this will affect you during or after your lifetime. Regardless of what you call it, though, we all affect each other through our actions or our inaction. I am not a great spiritual thinker; however, this is basic.

On the Other Side we all know that one cannot take action without affecting the whole on a universal scale. To me this is the definition of God or, at least, as close as I can come to explaining the unexplainable. It is a complex system of checks and balances. Just like the scales of justice, the goal is balance and harmony.

As a human being, or even as a soul on the Other Side, it can be profoundly hard to feel that you're part of a collective. But the truth is that we can't separate ourselves energetically from each other. That's why you and I can communicate with each other even though you are on Earth and I am in another dimension on the Other Side.

SL: Earlier in this interview, you asked for God's forgiveness. What did you mean by that?

LR: May humanity forgive me for the part I played. May history forgive me. May I forgive myself. May everyone I affected forgive me. That is all I can accept responsibility for; indeed, it is all I have to give. But please know I do give it with all my heart.

SL: Why does clearing your name on Earth matter?

LR: I just felt that I wanted to do this, and I confess there is some part of penance here. I felt like this would help restore balance. And maybe someone hearing this, or many people hearing this, will make a different decision because of it. Take action instead of inaction, right a wrong, or avert an impending disaster. Then it will have been worth it to relive a painful chapter in my own history when I didn't have to—to serve humanity in some greater, positive, beneficial, or helpful way, and to be of service.

I am glad I did this. It has been excruciatingly painful, but worth it. It has been cathartic.

SL: Are you saying that you did this so you could change the future?

LR: Yes, this is what I am saying. Now it's up to all of you.

Reflections

Leni Riefenstahl is a very complex spirit. She forced me to face my own fears, and I, in turn, allowed her to state her piece for the record. If you would like to learn more about her, she wrote an autobiography in 1995 titled *Leni Riefenstahl*.

My next visit was from the French seer and astrologer Nostradamus, who some believe predicted Hitler's rise to power 400 years before it happened.

CHAPTER 12

NOSTRADAMUS

Nostradamus appeared to me as if he'd come straight from 16th-century France. He was wearing an expensive-looking blue velvet cloak with gold trim, light-colored hose, and a flat-topped black hat. He had light brown hair, a mustache, and a pointy beard. His energy felt big and powerful, but he seemed more somber and serious than charismatic. I sensed that he was most comfortable using his great intelligence and resources to help and to heal people.

Michel de Notredame was born on December 14, 1503, in Saint-Rémy, France. While he was also an astrologer and physician, he is most known today for his work as a seer. One of Nostradamus's biggest fans was Catherine de Médicis, queen consort of King Henry II of France, who eventually made Nostradamus counselor to her son King Charles IX.

Nostradamus wrote several books of prophecies in the form of four-line verses called *quatrains,* using a mixture of French, Latin, Spanish, and Hebrew. His most famous work, *Les Propheties* (*The Prophecies*), grouped quatrains in sets of 100, known as *centuries.* Published in 1555, it was expanded and reprinted in 1558, and has remained in print ever since. While Nostradamus had relatively little trouble with the Roman Catholic Church during his lifetime, his prophecies were condemned in 1781 by the Congregation of the Index, a body set up by the church in the 16th century to examine books and manuscripts for heresy.

One of Nostradamus's most famous prophecies, Quatrain 2-24, seemingly references Hitler in connection with war and Germany:

> With the hunger of wild beasts they will cross the rivers
>
> Most of the country will be against Hister
>
> The great man will find himself paraded inside a cage of iron
>
> The German child [of the Rhine] will see nothing.
>
> (Source: Reading, Mario. *Nostradamus & the Third Antichrist.*)

Perhaps lesser known, there also seems to be a prediction of Princess Diana's death within Quatrain 2-28. It is thought to refer to Dodi Fayed, who died along with Diana in a car crash while fleeing paparazzi. His father is Mohamed Al-Fayed, who shares his name with the prophet of Islam:

> The last but one, of the surname of Prophet,
>
> Shall take Diana for his day and his rest.
>
> (Source: Roberts, Henry. *The Complete Prophecies of Nostradamus.*)

As a physician and apothecary, Nostradamus was known for his novel treatments, including progressive hygienic practices. However, in 1534, he lost his wife and two children, presumably to the plague. He later married a wealthy widow, Anne Ponsarde, with whom he had six children.

Nostradamus suffered from gout throughout his life, which turned into dropsy, also known as edema—the abnormal accumulation of fluid in the tissues or in the body cavities. It can result in swelling and congestive heart failure. When I asked Nostradamus his cause of death, he showed me an image of fluid in his lungs. He died on July 2, 1566, in Salon, France, at the age of 62.

The Interview

Susan Lander: What would you like to talk about today?

Nostradamus: I would like to speak on prophecy, fame, and what I think now.

SL: What made you write your prophecies?

N: Sometimes you just do what you do because you have to. I did prophecy like I breathed, irrespective of the consequences. I produced my quatrains at my own peril; nevertheless I did them, because I felt that God wanted me to do them. I felt that they were Divinely inspired.

SL: Are you proud of the work you did?

N: Which work? I was also a doctor.

SL: Was that how you thought of yourself?

N: I was a seer, but I was a physician, too. I liked to heal people. I still do.

SL: Really? Is that what you're doing now on the Other Side?

N: Yes, working on medical advances. *[laughs]* We do not have to stay locked in the era of leeches as medical treatments, as during my lifetime as Nostradamus. But we did the best we could at the time. *[sighs]* I studied and studied; we all did. There was so much we didn't know. A sense of futility was our constant companion back then, and so much was a mystery. We learned and succeeded by so much trial and error.

Communication and the sharing of information was so hard back then, too. We all had to "reinvent the wheel," so to speak, each person starting from scratch with research before knowledge became widely disseminated. Now information gets shared in the blink of an eye—even faster than the blink of an eye.

At this point in history we have accrued more knowledge, but there is still so much we don't know. Can you imagine a world without disease? *[He is sending me a feeling of wonder.]* Amazing. Incredible! That is what we healers are working toward on both sides. Though illness and infirmities do serve evolutionary and soul-lesson purposes, I feel that people's time on Earth could be better spent in ways other than trying to frantically stay ahead of the latest diseases.

I am glad there are so many who have picked up and carried the reins of the medical profession. I would have enjoyed living at this point in history, being a healer, using the latest tools to help people.

SL: Tell me about your predictions. Did you always receive them?

N: Yes. As a youngster they were frightening. *[He is showing me visions of huge flames.]* At the beginning I thought they were just bad dreams, but then I began to see them come true and understood that they were something else entirely. It was frightening to receive these missives from the future, and to see so many with dire consequences.

Quite a few of my prophecies did come to pass. I think that some events are predestined in a particular lifetime, and there is not much one can do about it. You might say that while there are multiple possible routes, you will always end up at the same destination.

Still, I felt that sharing my visions was my responsibility. I did not always like what I saw, but many people were forewarned, and I could rest knowing that this weight was off my shoulders. Sharing this knowledge did not avert every sorrow, but I am glad that I shared what I could. Doing so allowed me to feel peaceful in the face of the inevitable tragedies.

SL: Did you ever feel satisfaction at being right?

N: God, no. How can one feel joy at a tragedy that one has seen coming? It sometimes made me feel as if we were all giant pawns of the universe, and there was nothing we could do to change our destinies.

What I saw did not always come to pass. Sometimes there were random convergences of circumstances that changed outcomes. Maybe my actions sometimes delayed the inevitable. But as long as I lived authentically from my heart, I had peace and a clear conscience. I lived my life with integrity.

SL: Once you knew that you could see the future, did you intentionally ask for prophecies so you could warn people?

N: Yes. I will confess to a sort of morbid curiosity that coexisted with my not wanting anything tragic to happen. But we all have contradictions inside us, and this was no different.

SL: Do you have any words for those who seek to discredit you and say that your prophecies are false? Some say that your prophecies are manipulated and reinterpreted to make them fit with what happened.

N: I would say it does not matter. Those who want to hear, will; those who don't, won't. That is never my concern. I do hope that people will heed my warnings, as there is still danger afoot. But, again, all I can do is sound an alarm. That is all I have ever done.

SL: Can you give specific examples of where danger is afoot?

N: The Middle East is still a hot-button danger zone. *[He sends me a picture of a man in a turban I do not recognize.]* And beware of Greeks bearing gifts.

Continued instability in those areas of the world is a problem financially, socially, politically, and economically. When you think things are settling down and turn your back, that is when there is the most danger. Your government, and indeed the world's governments, should be mindful of that.

SL: What about North Korea or China?

N: North Korea, the quiet behemoth—very, very dangerous.
What goes on behind closed doors,
Guns blazing and the blood shall run.
Out of the North the savior, but very much alone,
[I am seeing Obama]
Will need allies stepping out of the dark.

SL: What about the United States?

N: Ah. A time of a great social change, prosperity, abundance. An Age of Aquarius. A reaffirmation of faith, although not in a religious sense. One warning: do not move backward in time. Guns and knives are the old way. Make a choice.

This concentration of resources with the affluent and the lack of clear priorities have led to a dichotomy in your society. Again, the people must make a choice. Until there is a more equal distribution of resources, there will continue to be misery, poverty, and widespread disease.

SL: The purpose of this project is illumination, and giving people who are here some new options and possibilities for their lives. What can you tell people that is illuminating?

N: *[laughing]* You honor me. It is not as if I am such a lofty thinker; I just have a higher perspective. Because I am "higher"! *[He is joking.]*

Illuminating . . . illuminating . . . I would like to speak with people about personal responsibility and encourage them to consider how they are using—or whether they are using—their own personal power.

I think that people suffer from feeling a lack of significance . . . yet people are all that *is* significant! Know your own power. Take your place in the grand puzzle that is the universe, for it is uniquely yours. Nobody else can make the difference that you make. I am a perfect example of this. I came here, I did what was uniquely mine, and people still remember me for it. Actually, they are still fighting about it, which, I confess, I rather enjoy. Was it this, was it that, was it right, was it wrong?

So my questions to all of you are: What is uniquely yours? What did you come here to do? What makes up that unique being that is you?

Write it down, appreciate it, and above all, never apologize for who you are. It is your magic. Live it, and you will make a difference—and you will enjoy yourself in the bargain. Do not listen to the naysayers and the fearmongers. Understand that what motivates them are their own personal fears. Leave them to their fears and move on. I wish you grace, I wish you much love, and I wish you a life fully expressed.

SL: I have one more question. How were you able to receive the quatrains? What was your process?

N: I could hear them, see them, feel them, taste them, smell them, and dream them. All with my sixth sense, or intuition, as you call it. I could sense or hear the phrases coming, and then I committed them to paper. I knew that they were very important. It made me cry sometimes to see what would happen. But I knew it was all I could do to document them and hope my writings would survive and warn people about the future. I am grateful that they did. The controversy that has always swirled around them has served to keep them alive and in the popular consciousness.

Again, the attention is flattering, but I was just doing what I did, like breathing. And there was a price to pay to see these events, wondering what impact they would have on society, and my descendants, for generations. Worrisome thoughts, for sure.

I am glad that you are all still on Earth, relatively well and thriving. Humans are a tenacious species, without a doubt. We cling to life, sometimes without even knowing why! That is a wonderful evolutionary trait. But there is something more wonderful about humans, and that is their need to alleviate suffering in others. That is why I kept a record of my predictions and passed them down as my gift to future generations.

There is an easier way to ensure your future rather than studying predictions and trying to stay ahead of random acts of terrorism—through a societal commitment to thriving and peace. It is up to each of you who are on Earth now. I cannot do that for you.

Select leaders who share your vision, for they are the handful who hold the cards. You are putting them in charge of the earth—your birthright—and their decisions will dictate your future in great part. You do not need my predictions to know that; you can see it for yourselves. Just open your eyes, open your mind, open your heart, and you will see.

Reflections

If you are interested in learning more about Nostradamus's prophecies, Mario Reading's book *The Complete Prophecies of Nostradamus* is a detailed, extensive resource. I can't help but wonder which of Nostadamus's prophecies are yet to be fulfilled!

My next visit was from a mystic of a very different sort, who came along 200 years after Nostradamus—Marie Laveau, the Voodoo Priestess of New Orleans.

CHAPTER 13

MARIE LAVEAU

Mystery shrouds many aspects of the life of Marie Laveau. Even her date of birth is uncertain; according to some sources, she was born in New Orleans, Louisiana, in 1794, while others say September 10, 1801. She could not write and did not leave a written record of her life. Much of what is known about her is gleaned from interviews with others as well as newspapers of the time. Legend has it that she was Creole and multiracial—her father was said to be a wealthy white planter, and her mother, his mulatto mistress; or she may have been the daughter of two free people of color. By most accounts, she was a hairstylist and a well-respected healer. The number of her children ranges from 5 to 16, depending on the source.

She was believed to be a practitioner of voodoo (also known as *voudou* or *vodun*), and she performed rituals, dispensed curses and cures, and sold *gris-gris* (amulets). She became known as the Voodoo Queen or Voodoo Priestess of New Orleans. It is believed that her daughter, Marie Laveau Paris, stepped quietly into her place during the latter decades of the 1800s, providing the illusion that she possessed eternal youthfulness.

She died on June 16, 1881, in New Orleans. Many make a pilgrimage to her tomb to this day, requesting favors and spells. According to her, the cause of death was, "Cancer. Old age."

The Interview

Susan Lander: Why do you think people are still interested in you?

Marie Laveau: Because people love a good mystery! *[She throws her head back and laughs loudly.]*

I love that people are still interested in me. The stories surrounding me are more of a fun thing, but they are accurate enough in ways that count. I have no desire to set the record straight! I would rather remain shrouded in mystery. *[smiles]*

I am not disrespecting vodun—that is the last thing I would do. It is a very serious religion and a serious practice. I believed in it, and I loved it. But those "supernatural" occurrences that were said to have been brought about by me? No, the forces that I used were "all natural," so to speak. I was an herbalist, and I also tapped into the forces of energy and nature to bring about change. People sought me out and paid me for that.

SL: Were some of these forces you used "dark"? Or unholy in some way?

ML: Do you mean satanic?

SL: Yes, that would be one type of dark force.

ML: No, they were not. People need to stop being afraid of their own power.

I think this is where the misconceptions about vodun come from. If people don't understand something, they tend to be afraid of it. If something isn't manageable, easily contained in a little box, it is scary.

We are beings of tremendous power and never-ending possibilities. That is what we need to understand. We don't have to pull away from that. We don't have to run from those who tap into the power of nature, the power of energy, the power of our thoughts, the power of our spirits. We do not need to be afraid of the unseen world or of the spirits who live there.

SL: Could you see spirits?

ML: Always, from the time I was a little girl. Some of my children inherited that as well. Especially young Marie. She was the one most like me in looks, gifts, and temperament.

SL: What did that world look like to you when you were here?

ML: I could see the bright sunlight and warm companionship of being on Earth and enjoy it. I could also see the spirits of the deceased coexisting with the physical world. They could talk to me, just like you are doing now.

I could also see fantastical creatures: dancing skeletons, things with sharp teeth. They did not scare me, though. I did not believe that just because a thing looked a particular way, it was necessarily that way. If I believed a creature could help a person, I worked with it; I tapped into and concentrated those universal forces of nature and made something happen. I understand that this may sound scary from your frame of reference. But from my perspective, it was never worse than looking at a creature that any of us could conjure in a dream.

You see, the universe has a wide variety of inhabitants, and many of them would love to help us in some way. These people, animals, creatures, gods, goddesses, saints, and angels are just sources of information and Divine intervention. They may act as our guides and helpers—but we do have to ask. They don't like to interfere with our free will. So you can, for example, light candles to particular saints to make a request.

I was born with a gift, and then trained to organize all of this and make it work for the benefit of others. I could help some to heal or help others grow rich by accessing the sources of abundance. I could bring the energy of romance or freedom into others' lives. Did it work? Usually it did. Did it matter when it didn't? Not really. I am not God. All I could do was set my purest intention to help and hope for the best, which I always did!

We are always asking for help. We are always trying to influence our environment. It is the human condition. But sometimes people just need a facilitator, and that is where I came in.

The beauty of vodun is that it works with the laws of nature, so it can affect all that is. Exactly how it works and why is very mysterious; I simply knew that it did work. When people came to me, the means didn't matter; it was the result that was important to them.

In your modern-day society, these concepts are much more mainstream. Consider energy healing, in which you harness the energy that surrounds you, and the Law of Attraction, the idea that we attract situations that we want or don't want through the power of our thoughts, feelings, and beliefs. People are no longer afraid to see those who talk with the spirits inside them; it is now commonplace. But when I was living on Earth as Marie Laveau, it was still so mysterious, and people were superstitious.

SL: There are accounts of curses that you supposedly placed on people. Are these stories true?

ML: Let me put it this way: I would occasionally try to break bonds between people if clients asked me to, if I didn't think there was a malevolent purpose. I had my clandestine ways of dealing with things if something didn't feel right. At the center of it all was a higher purpose. I realized then, as I do now, that certain things are destined and will happen (or not) regardless of my intervention. But if there was room to intervene and I thought it was for a higher purpose, I would not hesitate to try. There would always be some higher power between me and the final result, but I was good at bringing about change and facilitating the process.

A perfect example of my work is love spells—these were always a big seller! People so want love, more than anything else. A person would come to me, heartbroken, wanting to be with someone they weren't with. This is how my love spells worked: I could get them to notice each other, put thoughts of each other in their minds, connect their energies, and visualize them together. Then I would add some stones and herbs with the appropriate properties, and voilà! I loved helping love along; I had some good experiences with love in my own life!

I also loved using my skills to help bring about physical healing. In addition to spells, I studied the healing properties of plants as medicine. People have been doing that for thousands of years, passing knowledge down through word of mouth. That was how I learned. Again, it is not mysterious; it is a body of knowledge like anything else. You learn and you practice, and you see results. You learn what works best, like any doctor.

SL: Did you ever do a spell to bring harm to a person?

ML: No. To separate them sometimes, that was all. One must be very careful with curses and negative spells. They can easily bring harm to the practitioner if they're not careful. It's better to make good things happen for a person. Ultimately everyone is happier that way.

I loved having vodun in my life. I enjoyed working with it. I loved the mystery and having magic happening all around me. I loved living in the flow with nature, in harmony with the forces of the universe. It was a great way to live. I have no regrets.

SL: I understand that people still leave trinkets and offerings on your grave in New Orleans and make a wish. Are you aware of this?

ML: Of course! I think it is wonderful. A wish is the first step toward the manifestation of a desire. I think somehow people instinctively know that. The mistake they make is stopping with one wish! You have to keep wishing over and over, making your vision clear and precise. Do everything in your power to make it happen. You are here on Earth to make things happen! But most people know only how to start the process and don't know how to finish it. That was the part I facilitated. But people don't really need me—or any psychic, for that matter. Now, I don't wish to offend psychics and healers, and I don't wish to deprive those who make a living using their gifts to help others; it's just important that people know that they have their own power.

If I could give one message, it would be: Don't be afraid of your own power and what you can accomplish on your own. You must learn to have faith in yourself. Other people can help, but when you step into your own power, the desires of your will and your heart will take you a long way toward your goal.

The first question you must ask yourself is, "What *do* I want?" Most people don't actually know, which dilutes their intention, making it harder to manifest anything. Getting clarity on what you want and creating a pristine focus on your intention is the critical first step.

So you see, I was like one big, laser-focused manifestation machine. I may have had extra tools at my disposal, but don't sell yourself short. Use what you have.

SL: Thank you! Very interesting.
How do you ultimately want to be remembered?

ML: The same way I am now! Magical, mysterious Marie Laveau. I hope I haven't changed that. *[smiles]*

SL: Not a bit.
Did your daughter, who was also named Marie, succeed you as the Voodoo Queen of New Orleans?

ML: Oh yes.

SL: How did that happen?

ML: It wasn't a calculated thing, exactly. It wasn't like we sat around and decided to do that. I was just getting old and tired of my daily responsibilities. My daughter agreed to take over the business. And the story that it was still me but I never aged took wing, the way stories do. And that was that. People who knew us knew that we weren't the same person. But somehow over time, the myth really set in. We enjoyed maintaining our mystique, though. She is here with me now and agrees.

SL: Would you have liked to have done anything differently in that lifetime?

ML: I would have liked to further develop my capacity to love. Not only would it have made me happier, it would have made all of my relationships better. And it would have made me more powerful in everything that I did. I could have helped more people with love advice, too.

Oh well. We all have our lessons. That was certainly one of mine. I think that was why I was drawn to working with the energy of love, with love power and spells. I love romance and happy endings.

SL: How can we develop our capacity to love?

ML: Stop and think about what you are doing in your relationships. Be present, and enjoy each moment. Don't cast about, looking for what's wrong and who else might be a better choice for you. There is no such thing as a perfect fairy-tale relationship.

Watch how you treat people. Hold them within your heart. See them from the highest part of you—the part that loves unselfishly, that looks for the good rather than the flaws. It is easy to find flaws in everyone, but the truth is, the good far outweighs the flaws in most people. Look there. It is really just a matter of shifting your perspective; it just takes time and practice to make it a habit. I suggest that you commit to developing this skill. When you see others in a gentler way, they will be more inclined to see you that way, too. This can be the new, evolving thread that connects you, and it will very much improve your relationships.

SL: Do you have love now on the Other Side?

ML: Oh yes, this is a place of infinite love. It is where I drew my love power from to use in spells and in my own life while I was on Earth! The love here is pure and good, and pure love is devoid of evil intentions.

I have a gentleman companion here. We are very happy. I found what I was looking for.

SL: I'm happy for you! Do you have any other messages?

ML: I think I covered what I wanted to talk about. My central message is to love yourself and others. Realize what a powerful being you are in your own right. The world you live in is full of good and right and just possibilities for you.

Never be scared of things you don't understand. Just try to learn more about them, or at least allow the space for them to exist freely, without judgment.

Finally, never wish evil on another. That will never work well for you; evil cannot bring you good. I know this firsthand. Try to look for the good in others, and you will be better able to see it in yourself.

I am sending you all my love. See you out there in the universe! And if you ask me for something, I may deliver! *[She vanishes, smiling mysteriously.]*

Reflections

Given the lack of confirmed facts about Marie Laveau, it was gratifying to receive new information from the woman herself. It is clear, however, that she continues to embrace the mystery that surrounds who and what she was.

In the interview, Marie Laveau mentions the Law of Attraction. If you are interested in learning more about this, I recommend looking into the works of Esther and Jerry Hicks. Their book *The Law of Attraction: The Basics of the Teachings of Abraham®* is a great place to start.

Moving on from love potions to love poetry, my next guest was the equally intriguing ancient Greek poet Sappho.

CHAPTER 14

SAPPHO

This was definitely one of my favorite interviews. Personally, I found Sappho fascinating, and the myths that surround her, coupled with what she revealed in her interview, only add to her mystique.

We know that Sappho was born around 610 B.C. on an island in modern-day Greece, and died around 570 B.C. History did not record the cause of her death, but in her interview she said it was "something sudden and cataclysmic."

Sappho was a brilliant poet in her time. However, all that remains of her work today is one complete poem ("Hymn to Aphrodite") and approximately 200 fragments of poetry—beautiful verses about passion and love. It is unknown whether these poems are autobiographical. It is worth noting that the word *sapphic* was derived from her name, and the word *lesbian* is derived from the island of Lesbos, where she was born. I encourage you to read her poems and the interview to follow and come to your own conclusions!

We do not know whether she had a spouse, but evidence suggests that she had at least one daughter, named Cleis (Sappho told me it is pronounced "Clay-iss"). Fragment 63 of her poems reads, "A beautiful child is mine . . . Cleis the loved one . . ." Although some scholars feel that this may be a mistranslation or misinterpretation, Sappho suggested in our interview that she did have a daughter named Cleis, who died while she was young. She offered a new poem, "Love Beyond Reason," to give comfort to those who have lost a child before his or her time.

Along with several new poems, our conversation included very descriptive talk about lovemaking, which actually made me blush! But I enjoyed every minute of my time with Sappho, and I hope that you will, too.

The Interview

Susan Lander: What was it like to be Sappho?

Sappho: Intense.

SL: What was your favorite quality about yourself?

S: My big heart. My loving nature. Compassion.

SL: What was your least favorite quality?

S: Impatience. Seeking and restlessness. I was a wanderer. Maybe if I had been still for a moment, I would have let peace find me, as opposed to passing around me, over me, through me. True happiness, though, is what I sought. And I was convinced that I could find peace if I found true love—the love of another.

SL: Do you think this is the same of you today?

S: Absolutely. I am still seeking that which I sought.

SL: Even after all this time on the Other Side?

S: The soul's essence does not change. Our essential qualities, those that guide us, remain the same. Our central purpose in life, death, and life again remains steadfast. It is who we are. I think what changes is how we go about meeting our needs and how we treat other people. I am most often other-focused. I accept that about myself.

SL: Have you been back on Earth since your lifetime as Sappho?

S: Yes, many times. I was a Roman warrior. It was fun. I am quite passionate, and being a Roman warrior was a good outlet for that.

SL: You did not have a problem with the killing and violence?

S: That was my least favorite part.

[She shows me images of a smoldering battlefield, burned-down homes, women holding babies and standing alone.]

I remember all the blood and chaos. That tinny, metallic smell of blood. Wounded soldiers writhing in pain. That feeling of death and chaos after the fighting was over. As if all the gods had left and the glory was over—barren, with a feeling of emptiness. What was left? Mere mortals on the battlefield and the spoils of war. Women and babies, too. Slain, or widowed and left to fend for themselves alone. There was no honor or glory in killing innocent women and babies. It was not their fault they were on the wrong side.

Of course I have a problem with that. It haunts me to this day. Scorched earth, acrid smoke, and the smoldering timbers that were all that was left of people's homes. Charred skeletons where there had once been life.

It was hard to see the beauty even in sunshine on days like those. I remember standing on the battlefield and looking up at the blue sky and the sun, and wishing I could feel something good. Derive some comfort from it. But even the sun felt weak, as if all the violence had somehow divested it of its power.

But all the drama, the surge of energy, the pomp and circumstance, marching in tandem—it could be intoxicating. The powerful male body I had was very sensual, and inhabiting that body was such a rush. I felt so strong and confident. That is what I remember most.

SL: What other lifetimes do you want to mention?

S: The Middle Ages, that was grim. Dark. Dank. Devoid of the sensuality I love so much, that I crave so much. It was a life where you just had to get through the day and do your duty—bake the bread, wash the children, sweep the hearth, clean the kitchen. I was a woman, although I didn't think it was any more fun for the men. We all had to do our duty. Where was the fun, I ask you? Even sex was a chore. And for me, that is saying something.

I was happy to leave. I was just marking the days. Never again, something like that. Never! I think I wanted to learn humility and explore and inhabit a lifetime where there was less beauty, in order to find it within myself. I don't have to do it again, though; that is my choice. Sometimes it is fine just to be who you are, and explore deeper dimensions of that.

SL: Do you have any plans to come back to Earth for another lifetime?

S: Not right now.

SL: What is your life like on the Other Side?

S: It's fun, interesting, and stimulating. I am part of a community of women here. I enjoy that. That is whom I prefer for companionship. I do continue to write poetry, though, and plays and stories about my feelings. Some of my plays are produced for the public stage. That makes me feel good.

SL: So let's talk about your love poems, what you were and are so famous for.

S: It is amazing to me that something in my poems still captivates people so many years later. It was just my feelings transcribed on paper! I mean, papyrus. *[smiles]*

I barely understood the attention even then, but I enjoyed it, of course! It feels good to get noticed. But to me, it felt lightweight. It still does. It is just my own musings, the feelings of my heart. That people were interested back then—wonderful. But that they're still intrigued now? Incredible!

SL: Why do you think that your verses have stood the test of time?

S: I can't say, except that they must touch a common chord or people would not be interested. I must be striking at the heart of who we are in a very true and unusual way. I can see that intellectually, but emotionally it is a bit baffling and overwhelming.

SL: Are you saying that it's overwhelming to have people read them?

S: It makes me feel a little unworthy. Vulnerable. I do feel vestiges of ego from my Earth days. These writings are so personal, from my heart. But if it brings comfort and beauty to someone who needs it, that is a good thing, and I am okay with that. I cannot really do much about it from my vantage point anyway, and to be honest, part of me craves the attention.

SL: Did you love women in your lifetime as Sappho?

S: I loved everyone; I still do. It's just the woman-woman aspect that seems to capture my imagination so much. So much beauty together in the most intimate, erotic way. Aphrodite times two. It sizzles, and there you have it.

I am most drawn to women sexually, erotically, and emotionally. That is what is most natural in my heart. I share that with many women who love women primarily.

SL: I understand that many of your poems were lost. Please tell me about them.

S: They were all similarly themed and were about aspects of love in myself and others. One or two more poems may surface in the not-too-distant future. Some were not attributed to me that were in fact mine, and many others were influenced by me. But I certainly do not feel slighted! And I do not lack for attention.

SL: Do you think there is something unusual in the way you were loved, saw love, or loved others?

S: I think I just gave voice to people's feelings. Maybe in an unusually intense, precise, or poignant way. I revel in love; I want to bathe in it. Of course, this includes feelings of love that are nonphysical, for they are just as beautiful and can be just as intense! Great masterworks of literature and music are written about just that. And now they are being immortalized on film! Films are so wonderful; they awaken so many of the senses, and you can really indulge in the experience.

But my favorite is just getting lost and reveling in the sensations of the body—my own and others'. To lie next to another's creamy-white or honey-tanned skin and to taste it. Salty-sweet. Heavenly! Pure bliss. Truly one of the best things life has to offer.

I wish I could experience that now, but I can't, exactly, for I do not have a physical body anymore. At least, not at this time. I can experience very strong feelings and sensations, though, so my lovers and I can work with that and maximize the sensations.

[As Sappho speaks, she is sending feelings that are very intense, sultry, hot, and powerful. Her words pack a serious erotic punch!]

SL: So you have lovers on the Other Side?

S: Yes, many. Whoever will have me!

SL: Do you have a special soul mate on the Other Side?

S: Yes, but she and I are very free spirits. We come together from time to time when it suits us. I love her to the depths of my soul. She is the right hand to my left. We do not feel tied down, though. That would not suit either of us. We are really sexual, sensual, emotional explorers, exploring the depths through our interactions with others. It is who we are. So we are good partners, steadfast but not limiting.

SL: Did you have one special woman or man during the lifetime as Sappho?

S: There was one special woman whom I thought about the most, and who stuck in my heart beyond all reason. But I think it was because I confused her with Aphrodite! They were inexorably fused together for me somehow. When I was together with her, next to her, making love to her, I felt like I was loving them both in tandem.

It was very powerful and intoxicating! I think that's why I loved her so much . . . loved them so much! I think there is a little bit of Aphrodite mixed up in all of us. I think Aphrodite is part of us, in that place that loves and needs love so intensely.

SL: Can you give me a new poem? It does not have to be today.

[At this point, Sappho disappears and comes back an hour later.]

S:

Love is timeless, the most bountiful
Can you see what is in our hearts, immortal,
beautiful Aphrodite, and make it manifest?

The love we crave, the love that makes us whole
Do not stop before this creation is fully formed.

As we are one with our lovers
Let us be one with ourselves.
Divinely inspired, perhaps,
Yet perfection is always ours.
The love of another, the mirror reflected in their eyes,
Is what we should see.

Bountiful love, Aphrodite claims as her own
And delivers to our doorstep
Her most beautiful, tender, and eternal gift to each of us.
It is ours,
Love endless as time.

[Sappho is now high-fiving me. I cannot believe that she just gave me a new poem, the first in 2,600 years! It was a new experience for me, as I have never written poetry before. Once I recover, I resume asking her questions.]

SL: It is believed that you may have had a daughter in that lifetime as Sappho. Is that true?

S: Yes. She was so beautiful. She held my heart in her hands. It was from an arranged marriage when I was young. The union did not last emotionally. He and I divorced and went our separate ways eventually.

SL: Why did you participate in this project?

S: Because you asked me to. Once I heard of this project, I was intrigued. I would like to say hello to everyone in the modern world, to pop my head up out of the ancient world and make my presence known once again. It has been a long time since I interacted with the physical world, but I am still very much alive! I am not so different from the woman I used to be.

I want to give people hope. And to assure them, if they feel love-less, they are not! Love is all around you. In the birds and the flowers, the sun and the moon. Love is inside you now, all of you. You are made of it. I know it is hard to see sometimes but it is there.

Aphrodite is the embodiment of this love—a way of looking at it and connecting with it—but it is there either way. You don't need her in order to have it (with apologies to my beloved Aphrodite). It is indeed yours for the taking.

All my love to you, my most bountiful love.

[At this point I thought the interview was done. But over a month later, Sappho suddenly appears again and starts talking. She reflects on several themes that we had discussed in our conversation, concluding with poetic "musings" about love and a poem, "Love Beyond Reason," which she dedicates to her daughter.]

Musings

I do not know why
The heart craves as it does
Maybe it is seeking home
Union with itself
Through the love, life, of another.

All I know is that it is good, the best, a feeling like no other
That union between two souls
Moving as one

Rhythmically

In harmony

Bliss. The ultimate bliss.

Through my heartbeat

Through our hearts

I do not believe that it is an accident.

Are our hearts born to beat with each other, through

one another, entwined and in harmony forever?

I think so. I do think so.

So why can't we let it be, when we meet one, find one,

who meets these sweet and salty qualifications?

Maybe we are continuously seeking that perfect match?

That one who makes us whole?

Maybe it's God, only God that gives us that perfect match,

our eternal soul mate.

Or is it a collection of many that gives us that perfect one?

And in the meanwhile, I shall go on seeking.

Love Beyond Reason—an Ode to My Beautiful Daughter In Her Honor and Memory

The loss of a child

Before their time

A mourning and a grief beyond belief

A study in love

Passion like no other

Forever bereft of the call

To be their mother

Simplicity and complexity

All at once

The loss too much to bear

A hole in my heart

Forever undignified and empty

The hole that could only be filled by her

The longing that knew no bounds.

To all those who have lost a child too early

Before their time

And experienced grief beyond reason

Take heart and take heed

This child is still there

With you

In spirit

And life

Loving you forever.

[Again, I thought we were finished here. But a full year later, Sappho appears again, and delivers another series of beautiful poems.]

Studies in Nature:
Lilies
(For those with a broken heart, a journey in five parts)

I.

O lover, with your skin so white

The purest alabaster

Delicate as the whitest lily that

Only opens its petals at night.

II.

Come to me, my love,

Across fields full of lilies at night.

The stars shining overhead

Are witnesses to our love

As bright as the sky.

III.

O, the heart wants what it wants,

Imagining its perfect mate.

Alas, it cannot be so

Yesterday's heart has lost its mate.

So imagine the new one

With the trepidation that replaces the longing for what was

With what is.

The lonely crying—

the mourning doves never sounded so sad!

IV.

But know that the heart wants to love

And a new love will blossom

Filling that void with its rapturous beauty.

V.

Come to me, my love,

Across fields full of lilies

And all looks new tonight.

Possibilities

What are your dreams?
Bathe in a sparkling waterfall,
Water cascading off the cliffs
over your body.
Let the water wash you clean,
And start over.

It is the human condition to be afraid.
We fear what we do not know.

What you do not realize,
What you do not know,
What would change everything
Is the knowledge that you are eternal.
You are limitless.
Death cannot touch you, or touch your soul. Ever.
You are eternally alive, vibrant, growing, and changing.
Like a chameleon or the most beautiful butterfly.
You transform endlessly, every day.

Commune with nature.
Commune with yourself.
And dream.

How would you live your life differently if you knew this, really knew this?
Would you kiss more, love more?
Cry more, marveling at the beauty of it all?

Try more?
Take more risks, take more chances?

Can you dip one toe in the pool of possibilities,
and then dive in, reveling in its coolness and sparkling beauty?

Why can't you see your life as a child's game?
One full of unexpected twists and turns and possibilities
No judgment, only excitement.
What would you do?
What would you do?

Atthis, My Honeybee

My beautiful Atthis,
My honeybee.
Buzzing about me
To drink my sweet nectar at night
With her gentle and soft tongue.
There is no better communion
With nature.

My Story, in Retrospect

Longing, wanting,
Longing, wanting.
And Atthis wanted me.
And I wanted her.
And then she departed, as we all do eventually,
leaving me heartbroken and mourning.

At least that was the story.
My story, the story of "Sappho, the Lesbian Poet."

Endless stories.
Endless repetitions over lifetimes,
All sorting themselves out in Divine order.
But still, what have we learned?

On Earth we are just a cast of characters.
Names.
Faces.
They are no more than the cast of a play.
As the spirits who transcend the characters in this cosmic play,
what have we learned?

The lessons of love and loss, of poverty and prosperity,
of war and peace, of chaos, of compassion.
Of opportunities taken, missed, and tried again.
So take your place with grace
on the rich stage of the earth,
among the Divine cast of characters.
But never forget who you really are.

What is your role to play in this lifetime?
What led you down that road that came to Earth?
Transcend that act, that mask, that projection,
And let the light of your true nature shine through.

Fan the flame that burns within your heart.
Calling you to your Divine mission in your cosmic play.
It may be small or it may be grand, but it is yours.
When you find it, when you finally live it, you will know it.

You will find peace. You will find love. You will find happiness.
All will fall into place.
There is no finer aspiration, no higher pinnacle,
than being your own best creation.
And in doing so, you can change the earth.
You can change the world.

So show the world who you really are.
There is no need to be afraid.
Be brave.
You are full of untapped courage, and the talents and
abilities of a thousand lifetimes.
They are waiting for you to notice, and when you do,
they will burst into full bloom.
They are waiting.

Who are you right now?
Are you playing the character of this lifetime?
Or are you being the soul you are forever?
It is your choice.

What Lies Beneath

That heart-light
That beacon
Those windows to the soul.
Something, that intangible, unreasonable longing,
beckons me home.

What mysteries lie beneath, my new love?
It is dark, and I cannot see.
But nevertheless, I choose,
And I choose you.
Why would I choose you, not him, and not her?

Your beacon calls me,
Inviting me in:
See my mysteries, the Siren sang.
What lies beneath?

So I went to you.
Lured by your mysteries:
Your beautiful red hair
Your full ruby lips
The hint of curves beneath your mermaid's sheath.

And now we set out to navigate the watery seas
we have created together.
Its footing elusive, its depths unknown.

Will the waves be stormy and intense?
Or will they be calm and tranquil, lapping over us gently?

We can never know when we make that choice.
Will we find ourselves on those jagged rocks again?
Or have we finally found the one with that heart-light
Who will guide us safely home?

Reflections

The experience of working with Sappho challenged me as a writer and as a medium. I have written countless words over the course of this lifetime (as well as many other lifetimes), but I have never composed poetry, nor have I ever participated in creating anything so beautiful. It was an incredible honor to have collaborated with Sappho. Neither of us could have made it happen without the other.

Although I wouldn't call myself a romantic, while I was writing with Sappho, I felt she drew me effortlessly into her world—one that is completely guided and defined by love. Gentle love, sultry love, burning love . . . whatever the type of love, somehow she had me believing that *love* is all that matters. I love having her new poems to read because they take me right back into her world anytime I wish to go. I hope to take her depth of passion with me into all of my own relationships.

I have a strong feeling (and a fervent hope) that she and I are not finished writing poems together; I'm looking forward to writing them with her whenever she's ready.

If you would like to read Sappho's surviving poetry, you can find many translations available online for free. Check out the Project Gutenberg website at www.gutenberg.org; I recommend *Sappho: One Hundred Lyrics*, beautifully translated by Bliss Carman. To see the original Greek side-by-side with an English translation, consider Anne Carson's book *If Not, Winter: Fragments of Sappho*.

Now we're going to fast-forward over 2,000 years to meet with an artist of another type—actor, comedian, and classical pianist Dudley Moore.

———————

CHAPTER 15

DUDLEY MOORE

When I finished interviewing Sappho, I knew that my next participant would be Dudley Moore. Although it seems like it would be jarring to go from one interview with Sappho to the next with Dudley Moore, it was actually kind of restful. She had a very intense and vibrant energy, while his energy was much calmer. He was also very warm and full of heart, although I knew he wanted to talk about something that had been very painful to him.

Dudley Moore was born on April 19, 1935, in Dagenham, Essex, England. An award-winning actor, musician, and comedian, he starred in many successful British and American films, including *Bedazzled* (1967), *10* (1979), and *Arthur* (1981). He composed musical scores for films and for the Broadway and London stage. He also starred in a TV comedy series in the UK called *Not Only . . . But Also*, with British actor and entertainer Peter Cook (who made a cameo appearance in this interview).

In the 1990s, he began slurring his words, losing his balance, and having trouble remembering his lines. Some people mistook his symptoms for drunkenness, and his film career began to decline. It wasn't until 1998 that he was diagnosed with a rare neurological disease called progressive supranuclear palsy. This condition ultimately led to his passing on March 27, 2002, in Plainfield, New Jersey, at the age of 66. He told me, "I was ready to go. It was not a good way to live. It had long since ceased to be fun."

Shortly before his death, Moore was honored as a Commander of the British Empire at Buckingham Palace. He still cherishes this award.

He was married four times and had two children, and was also linked romantically with some of Hollywood's most beautiful women. At one point he was rumored to be dating the statuesque blonde actress and singer Susan Anton, whom you may remember as the gorgeous "Muriel Cigar Girl" from her commercials in the 1970s.

When it came time to do his interview, though, he got right down to business.

The Interview

Dudley Moore: I would like to talk about life as a star with a chronic illness, and what it was like to be thought unreliable because of it. Then I want to share some thoughts about the life I lived, and leave you with some suggestions on how to make your life better now.

Susan Lander: Can I ask you a few questions first? I had a few ready for you.

DM: Yes. *[smiles]*

SL: What was your favorite quality about yourself?

DM: Love. I loved women, especially! And that I could play beautiful piano. I miss my piano.

[He shows me an image of him playing a grand piano, and I hear music.]

SL: Your least favorite quality?

DM: Ego.

SL: What made you compose music?

DM: What can I say, you do what you do.

SL: Do you have any regrets about the way you lived your life?

DM: None, although I wish my health had been better so I could have lived longer.

SL: What was it like to be you when you became a star?

DM: Grand, of course. It was a high. I loved the fun and the access. But at the same time, I understood that it was just another movie set. The real deal is who you are, who your friends are—are you happy, do you like your life? Do you like the way you feel when you're in it, all aspects of it?

I'm not knocking it. Most of the time I did like the high life, and sometimes I absolutely loved it.

SL: Why Susan Anton?

DM: Ah, why love? Isn't that the question?

[I see and hear him playing the grand piano again.]

SL: Do you think there was a change in the way you loved over the years?

DM: It became deeper and truer as I got older, and so much more precious. I think I appreciated it more on a deeper level. We all seek love, both on Earth and on the Other Side. We are magnetically attracted to its magic. It is easier to love from where I am now.

All is love. All is forgiven. Love is sparkling and endless, reflecting who we are like the sea.

[He shows me an image of the sea sparkling in the sun.]

SL: You said you wanted to talk about living with chronic illness, particularly how it is to be a "star" with a chronic illness.

DM: Well, at first everyone thought I was drunk—a drunk! That was hard. It took a while to decide to come out as one who had a chronic illness, particularly one that I knew would eventually kill me. At the time, I wasn't sure which death sentence would be worse: one for my career, or one for my life. At the time I thought it was one and the same.

It is almost easier in Hollywood to be an alcoholic. You go into rehab, get fixed, and you're done . . . at least until the next time, God forbid, it happens. People can understand that. They aren't afraid of that. That's business as usual. But if you're sick, watch out. They're afraid you're going downhill; you're done, dead. No one will work with you. It's about their own fears, of course. But still, there it is.

Worse still are those who feel sorry for you and fawn over you. You want others to be genuine. You want to stand on your own as who you are, not to be treated as a child. I wasn't a child; I was just sick. But the inevitable ultimately happened, the downhill slide, and I watched my personal and professional life ebbing away.

Please don't get me wrong; I'm not bitter. I had a long, fun run, and my life was mostly good, as I remember it. I feel it's human nature to be scared of death. People shy away from it as if it's something they could catch. I am here to say, you can't catch it, but you can't hide from it either, so you might as well tolerate it. Treat those who are ill with respect. People who are sick, especially those with terminal illnesses, often gain rare and precious insights into life at the same time they're facing death. And this means they have something valuable and beautiful to offer the living.

SL: Do you feel you were treated badly or disrespectfully as you became sicker?

DM: I know it wasn't intentional. People tried to be normal with me. But it was very hard, and I sensed their struggles in dealing with me. Nobody wants to be condescended to, and I used laughter to hide the tears and pain that were inside me. My art, my music, and my song sustained me—*they* could never betray, never condescend.

My identity as an artist and musician was always very strong. So even when I lost my faculties and abilities, I still knew who I was, and I respected myself for that. I was a really serious, sensitive person inside. Like I said, I could cover that up with laughter. But inside I was very forthright, stalwart, and steady.

I'm not discounting the fact that I loved to make people laugh! I was good at that. I still am when I'm not being serious.

SL: So are you a stand-up comic on the Other Side?

DM: No, but I play one on TV. *[smiles]*

SL: What are you doing over there?

DM: Composing music, mostly. Writing plays for the stage. I still love to make music—music is God's language. I spend time with other artists and musicians. I feel great. I am happy and at peace.

SL: Do you still spend time with your good friend Peter Cook?

[He shows me an image of the Other Side: Dudley is sitting at a piano, and Peter is standing next to him. Peter is tall and lanky and wearing a rust-colored turtleneck in a style from the '60s or '70s.]

SL: I'll take that as a yes. Do you have a soul mate on the Other Side?

DM: Yes, I have a ladylove! She is beautiful. She is my destiny. She is my reward for going through the bad stuff. She understands me and loves me unconditionally. She is who I always wanted. I'm so happy a schlub like me ended up with someone like her! I'm always amazed that she wants to stick around, but she does. Go figure! She says I'm interesting enough to keep her interested.

SL: In retrospect, how do you feel about the life you lived on Earth?

DM: It was an intense one. It would've been much easier to have been invisible, although if I had chosen that path, I would not have been fulfilling my destiny. I came to Earth to be famous and to bring some lightness to that world amidst the tragedy. I think I accomplished what I came to Earth to do, so I am happy.

SL: What did you think about being given your royal title?

DM: Wow, I didn't see that coming at all! It made me feel truly humbled. I loved my country and my countrymen with all my heart. It was truly a great honor. I still cherish that moment. For a Brit, there is no greater honor or vote of confidence. Coming at that time, when I was so sick, it made me feel that I had done something significant and would not be forgotten.

SL: Do you have any advice to give to artists?

DM: Well, this applies to everyone. It sounds clichéd, but appreciate the moment. I am an example of how everything can be snatched away from you in your prime. I don't mean for this to scare you. I just want you to see that all you have is now, so love your life, and live it now. That is the opportunity that we're given in each moment. Don't live for your future; live for your present. Is there someone you want to love? Love them now. Is there something you want to do? Do it now. Is there something you want to say? Say it now. Now, now, now. Now is all there is. The future may be taken away or may take shape very differently than you had imagined.

My advice is to imagine the best life you can at the moment, and then try as hard as you humanly can to live it. Then you can rest easy when you go to bed every night, knowing that you're walking your path and fulfilling your destiny. Destiny can't always be found at the finish line, you know, but also at each stopover along the way.

SL: Is there anything else you would like to say?

DM: Take each hurdle easily. Take it peacefully. It's part of the life process. You'll get there if you follow your heart and prioritize what's important to you, whatever that is. Never sell yourself short. Never sell out your dreams. Keep striving. And remember to keep smiling.

My love to you all, especially those of you who were important players in the comedy/tragedy/musical that was my life. You know who you are, and I will never forget you. I carry you with me in my heart always, and I will see you again.

And to all of you: I wish you love, I wish you peace, and above all, I wish you a life well lived.

Reflections

Whenever I think of Dudley Moore, I think of him laughing and happy-go-lucky. This interview definitely shed some light on his more private self, which was very thoughtful and serious. It made me sad to hear about his journey after he was diagnosed with progressive supranuclear palsy, but I was glad he chose to come back and share his insights. I particularly liked his advice at the end, which came through with great strength, steadiness, and a feeling of peace: act now, live peacefully in the moment, and never forget to smile.

During the interview, his mentioning the sea as well as show-ing me an image of the sea felt like he was pointing me toward something. It only took a minute on the Internet to find it: Dudley Moore narrated the television series *National Geographic's Really Wild Animals,* which included the episode "Deep Sea Dive" in 1993. Working with spirits is always full of surprises!

The next interview was with someone I didn't see coming, but who also lived to make people smile: Walt Disney.

CHAPTER 16

WALT DISNEY

I was expecting someone else the day that Walt Disney showed up. He felt upbeat and enthusiastic, like a child at heart, and was dressed in khaki slacks and a sports jacket with a tie. He settled in, lit a cigarette, and politely refused to leave unless I agreed to include him in this book. As you can see, he won, in the process displacing a very famous poet to a *Conversations with History* sequel. I still feel guilty about it.

Walter Elias Disney was born on December 5, 1901, in Chicago, Illinois. Along with his brother and business partner, Roy, he founded what is now the Walt Disney Company. He was a pioneer in the field of animation. The characters that he and his company developed—most notably Mickey Mouse, whose first appearance was in the film *Steamboat Willie*—have been beloved by generations.

He planned and built two huge, world-famous amusement parks: Disneyland, which opened in 1955 in Anaheim, California, and Walt Disney World, which opened in 1971 near Orlando, Florida. Sadly, he died before Walt Disney World was completed. Other Disney theme parks have opened since then in Paris and Hong Kong, as well as numerous resorts and a Disney cruise line.

He died of cardiac arrest due to lung cancer on December 15, 1966, in Los Angeles, California, at the age of 65. According to Walt, "It was too soon. I wish I could have lived to see my grandchildren grow up."

The company Walt founded remains a leader in animation and developing new technology. But Walt's most important legacy may be that he changed people's lives and allowed them to believe in magic. So here is my conversation with Walt Disney (with apologies to my displaced interviewee, Edgar Allan Poe).

The Interview

Susan Lander: Hello, Mr. Disney.

Walt Disney: Call me Walt.

SL: Thank you, Walt. What would you like to talk about?

WD: I would like to talk about my legacy and about being a change agent. I would also like to leave some messages for my family and Disney workers.

First, there is some misinformation that I would like to clear up, once and for all: No, my body is not cryogenically frozen. And no, I am not a Nazi. I did not, and do not, support hate or intolerance in any form. I am not in the business of causing people pain or anger, or excluding anyone. I just want to give people joy. It's that simple.

It hurts my family that some misunderstand me, but they and I know that the majority of people love the legacy I left. It is as if part of me is still alive on Earth. Every time someone walks through the gates of one of my parks, gets on a ride, or stands in front of Sleeping Beauty or Cinderella Castle, they see me. They connect with me. I loved that then, and I still love it now. When I see children's faces light up, it feels so good! I will do everything in my power to allow their joy to continue.

I walk the streets of my parks and look at all the new inventions. Sometimes I sit in the screening rooms and watch old films, such as *Steamboat Willie*, as well as the new Disney creations. It makes me feel satisfied and nostalgic for the life I led here.

Never underestimate the impact your life can have, even after you leave Earth. Be mindful of your legacy. Seize the moment, I tell you. See what you can build. See what you can accomplish.

SL: Why did you want to participate in this project?

WD: To help people understand how much they can accomplish if they simply set their minds to it. It is so important to give yourself a goal, whatever that is. Just do something, fulfill a dream. You won't regret it!

I also want to talk about joy, and how underrated it is. For too many, life is just so much drudgery. We did not come here only to work. We must have fun, too. It is our birthright as human beings and as souls. People need to take a step back and look at the bigger picture.

SL: What is the bigger picture?

WD: People must have balance. People tend to take things too seriously. Yes, as souls we come to Earth to learn, but we're supposed to have fun in the process.

SL: Who is your favorite Disney character?

WD: Mickey, of course. He's such a little gentleman, but fun, too. People wonder whether I based his character on myself, and there is certainly some of me in him. But in any case, Mickey is an old friend of mine. He started it all. That's why I love him.

SL: Which Disney film is your favorite?

WD: Of the old-style films, that would be the original *Fantasia*. So magical. When you watch Mickey as the sorcerer's apprentice, you wish you could do that. It almost makes it seem possible, too. Don't we all want to wave a magic wand and make things happen?

SL: If you could wave a magic wand and make something happen, what would it be?

WD: To eradicate poverty. To make all of the children happy, to make them smile. To make sure that they didn't have any reason to be sad.

SL: I can see that you like to talk about magic. What is your relationship with magic? Did you believe in magic while you were on Earth, and do you believe in magic now?

WD: Magic has acquired an additional dimension for me now. When I was on Earth, magic was about a sense of possibilities. It was about a feeling of wonder and awe about our world, but more from the perspective of an observer than a participant.

When wonderful things happen and we don't understand why, we call it magic. But now I see that *we* are the essential ingredient in magic, and *we* are the cause of magic in our reality. It's not only something that happens *to* us; magic is a two-way street! Want, hope, and believe—and you really can make it happen.

Can you wave a wand and have something manifest just because you want it to? Probably not. But can you imagine some new technology, some new invention, and make it happen? Maybe you can! This is where you add your own magic, a dash of hard work, a pinch of this and that, and some luck . . . mix it together in a cauldron . . . put on your blue hat with gold stars . . . dance to wonderful music . . . wave your magic wand . . . and voilà! *[smiles]*

Never—and I mean never—underestimate your potential. Those on Earth are so quick to say "I can't" and find reasons not to try. At least say "maybe I can"; then use your imagination, and *try*. All great inventions are born that way. Then, when they come into this world, we call them magic. But the truth is, they are just imagination and hard work.

SL: What inspired you to build Disneyland and then Walt Disney World?

WD: My children. All children. I wanted to build a beautiful place for them to go. It grew from there. It didn't matter where. If it's beautiful, if it fills a need, people will come. You may have noticed!

As for the location, I loved that there was something wild, untamed, and expansive about the orange groves I decided to build Disneyland on—something to be conquered amid the beauty of nature. I believed that we could live in harmony with the environment and the oranges!

SL: What are your favorite rides?

WD: The carrousels, with their beautiful regal horses. Also, I do enjoy the rides with gentle roller-coaster areas—just enough to give the rider a thrill, but not really scare them.

The Submarine Voyage ride, which is no longer in existence, was a wonderful fantasy of what you might find in an undersea tour. Remember, back then we didn't have instant access to underwater or aerial views like you do now. Then, when the concept of that ride became outdated, it was replaced.

SL: What do you think of Michael Eisner, the former chief executive officer of the Walt Disney Company? I read that, although he was very successful in his position, he was also controversial and clashed with some of the top management, employees, and shareholders.

WD: Oh, you know, I'm not gonna answer that one. Everyone has their own vision and path to walk. I will never fault him for carrying out his own vision. We are different people, different spirits.

SL: What about the current chairman and CEO of the company, Bob Iger?

WD: No comment. It's his job now, not mine. Just keep up the magic, buddy.

SL: What do you think of Pixar Animation Studios? I read that Pixar had been in partnership with Disney before being purchased by the company in 2006, and that they are pioneers in developing and producing computer-animated films.

WD: Although I was not there directly, I still feel I somehow had a hand in building it. All of us at Disney have built and expanded upon each other's ideas, though there is still ample room for individual creativity. Imagineers are Imagineers—what we do is imagine, then bring our visions into reality.

SL: Would you recommend the use of the newest technology available today? Would you phase out older technology?

WD: I'm all in favor of using the latest innovations. I want to give the viewer—the consumer—the best possible experience. Why not keep up with the Joneses?

SL: Are you aware of all the movies your studios release these days?

WD: Yes, some. I like to pop in and out and catch bits of them. You know, I was watching *Monsters University* with you the other day.

SL: Yes, I did have a vision of you sitting at the end of the row in front of me, smoking a cigarette. Don't you know you can't smoke in movie theaters these days?

WD: *[smiles]* Well, they sure can't catch me now, can they?

SL: I guess not! What did you think of it?

WD: It was truly amazing and funny. Visually it was stunning—a product of the times, made with cutting-edge technology.

SL: There is so much violence and bleakness in movies these days, though. What is your opinion about these films?

WD: *[laughs]* I'm not going into that snake pit of a question! I'm not going to pass judgment on different genres. People have different tastes. The wonderful thing about modern technology is that it allows for many films to be made, quickly, for different sectors of society. I do believe that more is better when it comes to movies.

Sometimes, of course, a movie will be released that somehow shines brighter than the others, and you can never know what genre that will come from. That's the nature of the business. I'm not going to knock it, as a filmmaker myself. There is room for everybody, and a market for every kind of film.

SL: Would you change Walt Disney World, Disneyland, or Disney in general? If so, how?

WD: It doesn't matter; I have no judgment about it. Everything must evolve; it is the natural order of things. I step out, others step in. Others will follow, and they will make different decisions. That is how it should be. Stagnation would be the worst thing.

SL: But it seems that everyone who works at Disney must conform to specific standards in order to maintain a particular image. Isn't this counter to the concept of everything evolving?

WD: Listen, we are in the business of fantasy, and our characters are so well known. We are not trying to control the people who work for us. Rather, we are trying to preserve the fantasy for our visitors. We want a certain amount of consistency and predictability so people know what to expect when they come here. We don't want to disappoint them, least of all the children, who would be very dis-appointed if Cinderella suddenly became, say, covered in tattoos. I don't mind tattoos, but these are time-honored roles.

It is no different from actors playing historical characters. You can change some things, expand a bit within a framework. But we must honor the original vision. For example, look at the evolution of Mickey Mouse from *Steamboat Willie* to today. Different, but still recognizable—just modernized. Does that answer your question?

SL: Yes. I guess it does. Looking back, do you think the dreams you had for the Walt Disney Company have become a reality?

WD: It's an empire. I could never have imagined that my vision would have expanded so much and in so many ways.

SL: Are you happy with it?

WD: Oh yes!

[He shows me an image of a little boy's face lighting up as he looks at Cinderella Castle.]

This is all that matters. Is it making children happy—and adults, too? The framework doesn't really matter. I'm satisfied with what I created. My legacy is complete! It's wonderful, and I look forward to watching it all as it grows and evolves.

SL: Earlier in this interview, you said you wanted to talk about being a change agent. What would you like to say about that?

WD: People give me lots of credit for being a pioneer. But the truth is, we all have huge potential, and we can all be pioneers. If you choose not to do something, the only one standing in your way is you.

Now, I'm not saying that everyone comes to Earth to build a huge corporation—some do, and some don't. What I'm saying is, find what you're good at, what you're passionate about, and do it. This is the key to great success. This is where your power lies. Once you are working in your sweet spot, doing what you love, there is no better feeling.

I believe that most of us want to make our mark on the world. I am here to say that you can do that. Just believe you can. Know you can. Set your sights, set your goals, and go to it. No one else will do it for you. In this way, you can make great change.

SL: What about smaller changes?

WD: Don't underestimate the power of small changes to make a difference in the world. It's like the starfish story: A little boy is walking on a beach, and the tide has stranded hundreds of starfish on the sand. The boy starts picking them up, one by one, and putting them back into the water. A grown-up asks him, "What does that matter? You can't save them all." And the little boy puts one more back into the water and says, "It matters to this one."

You see, everything positive you do, everything good you do, affects hundreds or thousands of people down the line. Don't underestimate what you can do. You can be a change agent in that way.

SL: I never thought of it that way.

WD: Well, it's one of the main reasons I wanted to come today and share my messages. But also, I couldn't resist. I love participating in anything cutting-edge—new communication, new experiences. I'm like that.

SL: May I ask you about the Disney animators' labor strike in 1941? I understand that many of the top animators resigned, and it took a long time for Disney's work force to recover.

WD: No.

SL: No?

WD: No. I don't think that when most people think of me, they think of the strike. I have my legacy to protect, after all. I made the best choices I could think of in the moment. I had a lot of hurt feelings, and I know I hurt a lot of feelings during the strike. For my part in that, I ask for forgiveness. It is in the past. Let's look forward, always forward. Forward is where hopes and dreams can manifest into reality. Forward is where good, positive change can happen.

I want to take this time to thank all of the people who now work for Disney, and everyone who has ever worked for Disney. You always were and still remain my family. I have a message for each and every one of you: I hope you know that I love you and that I care about you. I always have and I always will. You are precious to me. I appreciate each of your individual contributions in carrying on the Disney name, the legacy, the idea of a better world for everyone. A world in which technology is used to make things better—I mean really better, and not just for profit. This is such important work. It shapes children's beliefs and will help them grow up to be productive, happy, healthy citizens of the world.

But most of all, I want to thank all of you for keeping the magic alive and for enriching the lives of countless children and adults. People still remember their first trip to Disneyland or Disney World. People feel real love for and connection with the characters. If it wasn't for all of you who continue this legacy, who continue contributing to the magic, that wouldn't be the case. You are essential to keeping the magic alive. So I thank you, from the bottom of my heart. Keep up the good work. Let your imagination soar. And never stop believing in magic.

I also want to give a message for all of my grandchildren (those I met on Earth and those I didn't), and the rest of my family. Goodbye and hello! I am here, and I am fine. As you can see, I'm still me. I miss you so much, though! I miss you every day. I miss being part of your lives. I am with my wife and my children. Roy is here, and we're all good. *[Roy is his son.]* We're all getting some well-deserved rest and recreation, but we see you and we watch out for you every day. We are glad that your lives have turned out like they did. We are so proud of you! I know there are challenges—that's just life. I want you to know that you are still so loved from the Other Side.

And to everyone reading this: love each other. And please know that the Other Side isn't so far away, although I know we seem inaccessible. Truly, we are only one thought away from each of you. When you think we are around, rest assured that we are.

SL: What do you do for fun on the Other Side?

[He shows me an image of a roller coaster.]

Are you saying there are theme parks on the Other Side?

WD: Of course. Why wouldn't there be?

SL: I have a few more questions. I understand that you were very interested in the future, and Epcot was originally envisioned as a city of the future.

WD: True. I didn't get to see it before I passed, but I can see it now, of course! I am very grateful for that. It is a mysterious universe indeed.

SL: What do you see happening with cities of the future?

[He shows me images of domed cities and wheelless cars that look like hovercrafts. The cars move by using underground electrical power grids.]

WD: Cities are very clean, very orderly. Barter systems are popular. There will be more equality, and wealth will not be as unevenly distributed. We will get back to a system that honors and rewards individualized initiative and accomplishment, but in a more balanced way. People will have more opportunities to get ahead, and the system will not be stacked against the powerless. People need to understand that this intense concentration of wealth at the top is counterproductive for us as a society.

Our strength is in our incredible diversity and the special talents that each of us has. One of the main reasons that we come to Earth is to develop these gifts and share them with the world. This will help move us forward so we can have the best society for everyone. It's harmful to have only a small sector making all the important decisions, to have only them expressing their gifts. It runs counter to who we are as souls. It is my hope that people will recognize that, and those in authority will realize that unchecked power is a corrupting and limiting force.

SL: Would you want to be living right now on Earth?

WD: Only to be with my family and friends. I would like to live in the future, though—maybe in a couple hundred years.

SL: So we'll still be here? No apocalypse?

WD: Here's hoping. That's up to all of you.

SL: Thank you.

WD: Thank you for giving me a chance to share my messages. That was fun!

[He shows me a hat with Mickey Mouse ears.]

And fun is what it's all about.

Reflections

Since the first thing Walt did was to refute two rumors about him, after our conversation I decided to do some research. I learned that there is an urban legend that his body had been cryogenically frozen. However, he denies this, and I was able to find two reputable sources to validate that he had been cremated: his death certificate, and his biography by Neal Gabler, *Walt Disney: The Triumph of the American Imagination.*

Second, some say that he was anti-Semitic, to which he replied that he does not support hate or intolerance in any form. The topic was addressed in the biography I mentioned; essentially, Gabler did not believe that he was an anti-Semite, further noting that Walt was a regular contributor to Jewish charities and had received a "Man of the Year" award from the Beverly Hills chapter of B'nai B'rith in 1955.

Moving on to more pleasant topics, I was curious about the term *Imagineers* that Walt had used in the interview. My search led me to *The Imagineering Field Guide to the Magic Kingdom at Walt Disney World* by the Disney Imagineers, where I learned that the term *Imagineering* was coined when Walt combined the words *imagination* and *engineering.* Walt Disney Imagineering (WDI) is the design and development branch of Walt Disney Company, the wonderfully creative team who builds the Disney theme parks, cruise ships, and resorts, among other things. So, as Walt Disney said, Imagineers do in fact imagine, and then bring their visions into reality.

For those of you who are interested in learning more about Disney history, www.thewaltdisneycompany.com is an excellent resource.

Just like Walt Disney, my next visitor, Eva Perón, jumped the line of other spirits who had been waiting patiently for an interview.

———————

CHAPTER 17

EVA PERÓN

Eva Duarte de Perón, better known as "Evita," showed up one day and seemed to knock everyone aside, like a bowling ball sending all the pins flying. She had on a camel-colored dress, and her blonde hair was neatly swept back and pinned. In my image of her, she looked like a formal painting, yet her presence was so huge and intense that I immediately gave in and did the interview; I knew that fighting her would have been pointless. That said, I was excited to talk with her. She is such a mythic historical figure, and it seemed to me that this spirit hadn't changed a bit since her life on Earth as Evita.

She was born María Eva Duarte on May 7, 1919, in Los Toldos, Argentina. She had a difficult upbringing, growing up very poor. Her father, Juan Duarte, was married to a woman who was not her mother, and he did not support his "illegitimate" family. He died when Eva was six, and her father's wife and family barred Eva, her mother, and her siblings from the funeral. At the age of 15, Eva left home and headed to Buenos Aires to find her fortune as an actress. She quickly transcended her background, becoming a stage, radio, and film actress, and starting an entertainment business.

In 1945, Eva married army colonel Juan Perón, who became the president of Argentina in 1946. She quickly became a skilled politician and a beloved spiritual leader. She redirected resources from the elite to workers, unions, and women, winning her many ardent supporters but also powerful enemies. In particular she had the support of the masses, who were called *los descamisados* ("the shirtless ones"). Through her Eva Perón Foundation, she gave out monetary aid and material necessities and established numerous hospitals, schools, orphanages, and homes for the elderly. She formed the Peronista Feminist Party in 1949 and was involved in the passage of a women's suffrage law.

She died on July 26, 1952, in Buenos Aires, at the age of 33. Even after her death, she remained an influential figure in Argentine politics as well as to her country's people. Her followers tried to have her canonized as a saint but were unsuccessful.

Of her cause of death, she said: "Cancer, but I wish it hadn't happened. Can you imagine what I might have accomplished? But my star is still shining."

The Interview

Susan Lander: How do you feel that your childhood shaped you?

Eva Perón: It gave me a great determination to rise above my circumstances. I had a strong drive to get out, to separate myself from that life. I did not want to be hidden. I wanted to be out front, a star. I can't explain it. It took me over and spurred me on.

SL: What lessons did you learn from your childhood?

EP: That there was never enough. To never settle for second best—I felt like I was less than proper, and it was a matter of respect. I had to get out and find my own man.

SL: I understand that at least some of the men you found were already attached to someone else.

EP: Yes, well, you know how it is. Maybe I was trying to reenact and solve the problems of my childhood. Very Freudian. I did succeed—and on a grand scale, I think.

SL: You were excluded from your father's funeral because you were part of his "illegitimate" family. How did that affect you?

EP: That was what steeled my resolve. That was when I understood my situation fully, probably for the first time. It was humiliating. Until then, my father was just my father. He abandoned us when I was a year old, and I was too young to understand. But that day, I really understood.

SL: Did you know you were destined for greatness?

EP: Destined? I don't know. I just had a burning desire for it.

SL: Did you have a plan for how you would achieve this?

EP: No plan. I was quite impulsive, really. But I did have good instincts and followed them. It was an upward trend. Up, up, up. I was lucky. I had my wits about me, but I was also smart. I don't mean to seem so calculating; I just knew which way I was going.

SL: Did you know what you were going to do once you got there?

EP: Not specifically. I felt that I had been treated with such injustice. I was filled with righteous indignation at my circumstances, and I channeled that into something good and helped others improve their circumstances like I did. I wanted to make the world more fair. There were those who had everything and those who had nothing, and I wanted to level the playing field. I was idealistic.

SL: Are you still that way as a soul?

EP: It's in me. At a certain level, we just are who we are. I want people to be good, I want people to be kind, I want people to be fair. I can't always have it, but I always want it. I will do what I can to help it along.

SL: If you came back and were born into similar circumstances, do you think you would do things the same way?

EP: The world is different now. But I would still rise up and conquer.

SL: Did you know how much the Argentine people loved you?

EP: Yes, I felt that. I was one of them, at a basic level, and they got that. And nobody in power was helping them to rise above their circumstances except me. So they were grateful. But there were those who hated me and didn't trust me, and that was hard. I couldn't understand that. I don't understand it. Why hate? It's such an unnecessary emotion. I never stopped trying to win them over.

SL: What would you say to your detractors?

EP: Go ahead, you try to do better than I did! There are always trade-offs. Of course, we want to be on the path of the righteous— at least, I did—but it's more complicated than when you have to work within a system. It can be messy when there are so many people, agendas, and social structures to contend with.

SL: Why do you think you had such support from the working class, unions, and women?

EP: I was them and they were me. We were from the same roots. I understood their struggles and their position.

SL: What do you consider your best accomplishment?

[I see her giving out loaves of bread.]

EP: Putting something in the hands of the poor, giving to people who need it—that was always my favorite thing. There is no substitute for direct touch and direct intervention. That always made me feel good. I was happy; I could have done that all day.

SL: But then you were taken early, at the age of 33.

EP: Yes. I was so frustrated! I felt like I was finally getting somewhere. I finally understood how to get things done.

SL: I understand that when you got sick, you didn't tell anyone until much later. Why?

EP: I felt like it was a sign of weakness. Looking back that seems foolish, I know. It would have been okay to be human. Maybe I could even have turned it into something good, something that would have helped people. But back then I was a star, and stars didn't get sick. It was unseemly. And I wasn't going down without a very big fight. I am proud to say that I held on as long as I humanly could.

SL: Did you think you were going to die?

EP: Not until near the end, when it was too late. Then I was very sad. But still, I have no regrets.

SL: I read that after your doctor diagnosed you with advanced cervical cancer, Juan Perón withheld your diagnosis from you and said you had anemia. Is this true?

EP: Yes, but I think he wanted to give me hope and be kind to me. I knew that I was really sick. It wasn't his fault. It was my own responsibility to take care of my illness, and I attempted to ignore it for quite a while. If I had addressed it early, maybe I could have been helped, but maybe not. We just can't know these things. Things happen the way they happen.

SL: I understand that after you became sick, you were given the official title of "Spiritual Leader of the Nation." What did that mean to you?

EP: It meant so much, but at the same time I was so sick that it was kind of futile. Still, it was like a beautiful kiss good-bye from my people. I cherish it.

SL: What do you miss about what you had on Earth?

EP: The food. Sex. Not much else. It was a tough place. The glory was good, though, and the moments of triumph. That was excellent. It made it worth it.

SL: I understand that there was a great deal of controversy about what happened to your physical body after your passing—it was moved around for 25 years before finally coming to rest in the Duarte family tomb at La Recoleta Cemetery. Do you want to comment on that?

EP: I think it is sad. I am not there, but I understand how sensitive the matter is. I honor the love and support of my people, and I continue to hold them in my heart. The body is just a symbol and no substitute for what is real between us.

SL: How are you different now from when you were on Earth?

EP: I like to think I am more tolerant of different points of view. I understand now that people are given hardships to learn, so it is wise to sometimes let things happen instead of trying to fix everything. However, we are also brought to Earth to learn to help people in need and treat everyone with respect. The power structure on

Earth is very rigid, and there is a tendency to get rich on the backs of others. If we can break through that, we can make the world a better, fairer place for everyone.

In answer to your question, I guess I still want the same things! But now I see the broader perspective; it is not so cut-and-dried, black-and-white. I understand that things can't be fixed in a minute just because I want them to be.

I think if I came back, I would pay more attention to love on an individual, interpersonal level. I think that I was too focused on the agendas of the moment. I had plenty of people I could have loved better! But I'm sorry to say that I didn't. I certainly felt passion at times—but love?

What is the difference between love and passion? I don't know, but I think there's something. To me, passion is everything. It eclipses everything.

SL: Did you love Juan Perón?

EP: Yes, of course. But, like I said, I could have loved him better. I was on a mission, and there was not much room for love on that level. I loved the Argentine people. They were my people, and I wanted to take care of them. That was my real *pasión.* I still feel so connected to them and hold great love for them in my heart.

Sometimes when things are bad, people need someone or something to unite them. I am glad I could serve that purpose and be there for them.

SL: Years after your death, Juan Perón married Isabel Martínez, who served as vice president of Argentina under him and then became president after his death in office in 1974. What are your thoughts on this?

EP: I am proud of her. That is a great accomplishment. Women should do things like this, break those barriers—there should be no barriers whatsoever! I wanted Juan to be happy, and if he found happiness with someone else, that is to his credit.

SL: Do you see him on the Other Side?

EP: Occasionally. We had a job to do, and we did it.

SL: Are you aware of the movie and play about your life, titled *Evita*?

EP: Yes. I've seen it.

SL: Seen what?

EP: The play. We can come and go, you know. *[smiles]* I was curious. Wouldn't you go see a show about your life?

SL: Yes, I believe I would! What do you think of them?

EP: Ricky Martin, now that is one beautiful man! *[He played the role of Ché, the narrator, in the 2012 revival of* Evita *on Broadway.]* I am flattered that people still care. This kind of immortality, living in some public way after one is gone, is really interesting and bewildering. But I am glad that I made such a mark that people want to keep telling my story.

SL: How accurate do you think they are?

EP: In a movie or a play, how do you fit a person's life into two hours and make it something other than one-dimensional? I appreciate that they tried, but that's hard.

In answer to your question, they got the broad brushstrokes right. Yes, I was ambitious, greatly so. That is me. I am driven in general to accomplish. Overall, they are quite romantic. I was still a human being. I had doubts; I had fears. I loved legitimately. I felt moments of great passion and triumph. Sometimes I felt so much pain, thinking that I wouldn't accomplish the things I wanted to. I worried that I would sink back into obscurity, open my eyes one day and wake up back in the town where I was born, and be that insecure, poor girl again. Believe me, I had such fears about going back there.

Still, I liked the shows, and it made me feel good to see them. I hope people enjoyed watching them, too, and learning a bit more about me. I like that an Argentine woman *[actress Elena Roger]* played me on the Broadway stage. That felt very honest.

SL: Why do you think people are still interested in your life? Is there a secret to your immortality?

EP: I think everyone wants to make a mark, to shine on some level. To rise up out of the depths and say, "Hey, here I am, look at me. I am not obscure."

I was a poor kid from an illegitimate family. If I could do it, anyone could do it. I think that was, and still is, my great connection to people. There will always be poor kids from illegitimate families. There will always be people who want more than they had growing up. If you can take that desire and channel it into a drive to succeed, that can be the secret to your success, too.

SL: Do you have anything else to say?

EP: Be unafraid in whatever you do. Live to your greatest ability. Always follow your dreams. Try not to judge yourself. As long as you are striving, you are doing the right thing, and you will be surprised at what you can accomplish. The world is waiting to see you.

My love to all, and deep, sweet *pasión* to all.

SL: Do you have any plans to come back? If so, what would you like to be?

EP: A world-famous scientist.

SL: Would you invent something—

EP: *[interrupting]* who would change the world.

Reflections

As I said, it seems that this spirit hasn't changed a bit since she was on Earth as Eva Perón. Everything she said was definitive and strong—no wishy-washiness there. She knows what she wants and isn't afraid to take action to get it. She is still incredibly idealistic and guided by a vision of a better world for everyone. I could really appreciate her perspective, as I am also an idealist with strong ties to the labor movement. I wouldn't mind having her on my team any day; whatever she put her support behind would likely prevail! If you would like to learn more about Evita, there is an excellent biography by Nicholas Fraser and Marysa Navarro titled *Evita: The Real Life of Eva Perón.*

Just as Eva Perón's story has been immortalized on stage and screen, my next visitor similarly lives on through his music— Louis Armstrong.

CHAPTER 18

LOUIS ARMSTRONG

I had the sense that someone was trying to communicate with me, but I couldn't figure out who; I just kept hearing the words *snazzy and jazzy*. The next day I saw Louis Armstrong! He was such a gentleman. He had a huge smile on his face as he tipped his hat to me, and I could hear his song "What a Wonderful World."

Louis was definitely "snazzy and jazzy"! The only problem was that I didn't have any questions ready for him. So I asked him to give me a few minutes while I called my niece Rachel, who is a musician. Fortunately, she came through with some excellent questions for me to ask.

Louis Armstrong (nicknamed "Satchmo") was born into extreme poverty on August 4, 1901, in New Orleans, Louisiana. As a child he sang in a boys' quartet and worked when he could, but in 1913 he landed in the Colored Waifs Home as a juvenile delinquent. Fortunately the home had a band, and it was there he learned to play the cornet. This was the era in which jazz was born, and it became his passion. He honed his craft listening to the pioneering jazz performers in the city and soon began playing in bands. He became known for his creativity and innovative musical techniques, and by his late 20s, he was famous.

In addition to his skillful playing of jazz, swing, pop, and Dixieland music, Louis was also known for his raspy singing voice and his warm, charismatic, and entertaining personal style. He was one of the first African-American entertainers to "cross over" and become a superstar in a country that was still racially segregated. His style, melodic complexity, and technical innovations set a standard for jazz, and he continues to impact popular music to this day. He released numerous songs and albums during his career, including *Porgy and Bess* (with Ella Fitzgerald), "When the Saints Go Marching In," "Mack the Knife," and "Hello, Dolly!" He was in over a dozen Hollywood films, usually appearing as a musician or a bandleader.

Louis died on July 6, 1971, in New York City at the age of 69. According to him, he died of a heart attack. He was inducted into the Rock and Roll Hall of Fame in 1990.

The Interview

Susan Lander: Hi, Louis! Did you always want to be a musician?

Louis Armstrong: People are born musicians. When I played music, such joy took over my body, and I felt it throughout my whole being. It was all centered in my heart. Why would I want to do anything else?

SL: What was your favorite song?

LA: "Winter Wonderland."

SL: Really? Why?

LA: It's like a beautiful little gem. So perfect. I love the snowy landscape, and the song is like that—smooth, cold, and crisp.

SL: Your music always makes me think of New Orleans.

LA: Ah, N'awlins! Music is the soundtrack of that city, what makes it tick, what makes it go 'round. You can dance down the streets, and no one thinks it's strange. I love that music pours out of the buildings, mingling, mixing. Gumbo, like its Creole heritage. Mixing it up.

SL: How do you suggest that musicians make their mark in music history using their own talents?

LA: Everyone has their own unique voice—like a fingerprint. Find it and you're home free.

SL: In other words, you don't want to be like anyone else.

LA: Yes, exactly. It doesn't matter what you do. You are beautiful just as God made you. Don't forget that.

SL: Do you feel being African American affected your career?

LA: Aah . . . music is the universal language. It brings all of us together. That is its greatest gift, I think.

When we come to Earth, people look different on the outside for learning purposes. But souls have no race; souls have no gender. And music cuts through it all, gets to the heart, the core, the kernel of truth at our center. When you hear my music, you hear my truth.

Music affects us all. We can't help it. Even those filled with hate cannot help but be affected. To them I say: Look inside yourself, and try to see how you are different from us, or from anyone else you think isn't like you. I defy you to find something really significant; you will see how futile an exercise that is. I hope people stop the hate, and start the love. Oh yes.

[I hear him singing and playing "When the Saints Go Marching In" on his cornet.]

SL: How did you gain the confidence to experiment with your instruments so you could find something that worked for you?

LA: Music was my savior. I had a rough childhood. It was my escape, my salvation. I kept going until it felt right. I knew I hit the mark when I felt that ping, that sweet spot.

If I could give advice to those studying music, I'd say the most important thing is to feel the truth in your body. That's how you'll know. It's like you're flying, soaring. Then try to remember what you're doing! But not too well, not too rote. You can even quash your originality by being *too* much yourself! Don't get stuck in a rut. Allow space for your originality and creativity. The magic is there.

Watch people respond. People respond to you being you because that's what special. If it's old, they've heard it before. There is something to be said about the technical perfection of the old masters, and students do need to learn the basics and have a solid foundation. But of course I'm more of a fan of free-form. It's more expansive, and I just feel it's easier to find the joy in it.

I take issue with teachers who encourage too much formula. It will be to the detriment of their students later on. Teachers, please give your students space to find their voice, and when they do, give them an A+! I was lucky. My teachers gave me space.

And remember to swing!

SL: I understand that you were one of the inventors of scat singing. What influenced your improvisational choices?

LA: I took a little of this, a little of that. And then just hit it where I was.

SL: How do you know where your strong points lie?

LA: Fake it till you make it. *[laughs]* Like I said, look for your strong points at your center. Where are you most comfortable? Where are you most free? Where is it most effortless? That is the strong point of all artists. When you're there, it's like breathing and it just flows. That is your power and your magic.

It doesn't matter what others say, because people will always have something to say. That's their problem. What makes you unique, what makes you special, is also what will make you powerful and successful. I promise you that. Find what you do well, and do it like you do. Success and personal happiness will follow.

I want to say something about that. What is the meaning of success? To me it means to be happy, to be grateful, to be graceful, and to lead a charmed life. But you got to start with the happiness piece first. All else springs from there.

SL: How do you lead a charmed life?

LA: Just see it that way. It's all a matter of perspective. If you are happy, if things are good, if you can find the love in your life, you'll feel like your life is charmed. And there's *always* something good to see or find in your life. Even if it's just going outside and looking at a flower or feeling the sun on your face. That's enough for me.

SL: Do you think a person can be successful without making a lot of money?

LA: *[laughs]* Oh yes, it's only so much Monopoly money. It's all well and good to have a nice suit, but you don't need that to be happy. When you're happy, you can play the best music. You can make the best music.

SL: You said you had a rough childhood. Do you want to talk about that?

LA: Not really. It's ancient history—long gone. I prefer to be happy. I choose to be happy. When I think of my lifetime, it's all about my music. That's what people remember. That's what I remember. That's what lives on and stays with me, even though I left Earth and am speaking to you from the Other Side. The hard lessons of Earth, such as ill health, tough families, and even poverty, don't follow you here. You may remember them, but what you remember the most are the good things you created. Your successes. Your accomplishments. Those speak to who you are.

You aren't your circumstances, your family, your fights, or your aches and pains. Sometimes things seem dark, but these times are transitory. They are not permanent, and they can't follow you to heaven. When you look back at your life from the Other Side, it's all about what you did, what you learned, and when you got things just right. That's what sticks with you.

Just be you. Be happy—it's a choice. Don't listen to anyone else's criticism of your music or your art. God is in you; find it and express it. You'll know when you're in that place and making that special music. That was the secret to my success, and it can be yours, too.

SL: Do you have any other messages?

LA: Please say hello to my adopted city of New York. I miss it.

Always be a true original, and never forget that your originality is what makes you special. It is your gift. Share it with the world and never look back. Go where your heart moves you; do what your heart calls you to do. Explore everything you want to try. That is an end in and of itself. Don't forget that the journey is everything. You don't always need to be focused on the destination.

Good luck and many blessings to all of you. May you find the ultimate success—which is to be the best you that you can be.

[I hear the notes of his trumpet solo at the beginning of "West End Blues" as he leaves.]

Reflections

It was wonderful spending time with this easygoing, upbeat, distinguished gentleman. I downloaded a couple of his albums and played them as we spoke, to set the mood. As soon as we finished, a song called "Sittin' in the Sun" started playing, which I'd never heard before. I couldn't believe the lyrics. It was about the true meaning of wealth—just what we'd been discussing.

If you would like to learn more about Louis Armstrong, his autobiographies include *Swing That Music* and *Satchmo: My Life in New Orleans.*

The music of Louis Armstrong made the world smile; my next guest, John Belushi, made the world laugh.

CHAPTER 19

JOHN BELUSHI

Finally, someone on my list actually appeared on schedule! I thought it would be fun to talk with John Belushi, and he did not disappoint. I grew up watching him in the original cast of *Saturday Night Live,* the long-running ensemble comedy show. I couldn't wait to see his over-the-top characters every week: "Joliet" Jake Blues of the Blues Brothers; Samurai Futaba, the samurai who turned up in unlikely places; and of course Pete, the counter guy from the Olympia Café, who refused to give customers anything but cheeseburgers, chips, and Pepsi.

John appeared to me in his overstuffed, striped Killer Bee costume from *Saturday Night Live,* complete with a red bandanna and antennae that bounced around his head on springs. He looked exactly like I remembered from the '70s, with his round face, dark hair, big smile, and scruffy short beard and mustache. He said he chose to appear "with a few extra pounds, just for the effect, because people knew me like that." He seemed a bit more serious than he used to, but I could tell that his brilliant, quirky sense of humor was still intact.

John Adam Belushi was born on January 24, 1949, in Wheaton, Illinois. He was an outrageous but affecting comedian, musician, singer, and actor. He began his career in 1971 as part of The Second City improv troupe in Chicago. In 1975, he landed his breakout role as one of the original cast members of *Saturday Night Live,* known as the "Not Ready for Prime Time Players," along with Gilda Radner, Dan Aykroyd, Chevy Chase, Jane Curtin, Garrett Morris, and Laraine Newman. He stayed with the show until 1979, and also starred in many well-known movies, including *Animal House, 1941,* and *The Blues Brothers.*

Fame eventually took its toll. He had a reputation for heavy drug and alcohol use, which unfortunately proved to be his undoing. He died on March 5, 1982, in West Hollywood, California, at the age of 33, after an accidental overdose of cocaine and heroin known as a "speedball." About his cause of death, he said to me, "Drugs. Not worth it." He was posthumously awarded a star on the Hollywood Walk of Fame in 2004.

The Interview

John Belushi: Hello! I thought you'd never make it. Thought I'd have to do this by myself.

Susan Lander: Ha ha, good luck with that!

JB: You need me, too. Without me, you'd have nothing but dead air. So I trump you, and I win.

SL: You have me on that one.

JB: I wish.

SL: Tell me about working on *Saturday Night Live.*

JB: Now that was the crew! We had such a good time! Those were the days. Gilda Radner is with me now, on this side. I'm sorry she is not with you anymore. I know her husband, Gene Wilder, misses her, and she misses him. Maybe she will talk with you sometime.

SL: I hope so. She was taken way too young, just like you were. I always think of her character Roseanne Roseannadanna on *Saturday Night Live*. What were your favorite characters to play?

JB: The Blues Brothers band and the Killer Bees were favorites, but I loved them all. They were really aspects of myself. Whether the character was comic or tragic, they all had a little something at their center that was me. We have all these aspects of different personalities inside us, waiting to come out. That's why I loved acting. It gave me a way to open the door and let them out. Legally. *[smiles]*

I am glad that audiences appreciated my characters and identified with them in some way. Even if I was a big dumb schlub, we all have a part of us that feels like a big dumb schlub.

SL: I have to agree with you there.

JB: Maybe a part of you wants to be a sleek, sexy blues player who gets all the girls, who travels and has fun adventures. People can live out their fantasies through actors' portrayals.

SL: Did you think the audience saw the real you?

JB: Oh, definitely. Parts of the real me, like a checkerboard. Aspects of me, hanging out on-screen for all to see.

SL: Was there anything you didn't show them?

JB: Yes. My vulnerabilities, my sadness, and my feelings of unworthiness. I didn't like them then, although now I know they're a normal part of life. If we don't understand who we really are underneath—that eternal, unspoiled, beautiful soul—it's common to feel that way.

I think we can't understand who we are until we're on the Other Side. That is the nicest part of it, really. We get to look at ourselves and say, "You know what, I'm okay, warts and all." We stop judging those parts we don't like, and see them as normal instead, as just as worthy of love as any other part of us—not only the "good" parts, the societally acceptable parts.

If there's one thing I hope for, it's that people would knock off judging themselves and each other. People can be so cruel, and it always hurts. Even when we pretend it doesn't and tell ourselves it doesn't matter, it hurts. My message is: "Treat each other nice! So says Big John. Or else!"

SL: Do you want to talk about your death?

JB: Passing, you mean. I just came up here, and I'm still here. I would have thought you'd noticed by now!

Thinking about my death, though, is kind of depressing. I had hit a wall. I was in a tough place, a dark place. But if I had waited or been more conscious, I think things would have opened up for me and gotten better. Sometimes when you think you're at the end of a road, it's best just to hang out there for a little while, because the light will come on and you'll see that the dark place was just a fork in the road. Then you can choose left or right. Life is set up like that. There will always be more choices, because nothing stays the same.

People are so funny. If things are good, they don't want things to change; and if things are bad, they do want things to change. But the truth is, we can't stop change. So I say, use this to your advantage. Always be curious and be on the lookout for the next cool thing. And if you don't like your life, change it, and that will open the door to more cool changes. 'Cause I can tell you, change is just around the corner, so look alive!

People love to play games, but they are so cautious with their real lives. I say, life is a game, too, so play it well! It doesn't have to be boring. (Video games, now—I would've loved that! You would not have been able to drag me from my Nintendo and Apple, had they been around in my day.)

You have the power to make your perfect fantasy life, just give it a chance. Seriously, I think that's where people go wrong. They're afraid to rock the boat, so they keep their lives the same. Do not cop out of your own life. Please listen to Big John. Live life to the max. Fly!

[Adding to his "fly" reference, he again shows me the image of himself as the Killer Bee.]

Here's the thing: I am bumming about the drugs. I think that was where I copped out, and it came back to bite me in the butt. Do I want to talk about the details? No, it's ancient history as far as I'm concerned. But I will tell you that there is so much danger in looking for happiness outside yourself. I don't care if it's drugs, sex, food, work—whatever. God knows, I tried them all. None of them stopped the pain. You can tell yourself it's fun, it's harmless, it doesn't matter. But the truth is, it does matter.

So the question you've got to ask yourself is: "Why am I using this?" Does sex feel good? Sure. Do drugs feel good? Sure. And please, I'm the last one to preach. But dammit, how many people need to destroy themselves with this stuff? Just check your motives. Are you using it as a Band-Aid for something—for life? Hey, sure, you can do that. It's ultimately your choice, and I'm not judging it. I'm just saying, you can get high on life without going unconscious.

The way I see it, you came to Earth to do something. Have you done it? Are these drugs or other addictions preventing you from accomplishing it? That's why they are so dangerous. They lull you into submission, into thinking they won't get in your way. Well, they sure got in my way, didn't they?

If I were still on Earth, I might have been a multi-zillionaire by now. *[smiles]* Made dozens of hit movies and had fun in the process. Made tons of cool new friends. Had the latest roadster. Enjoyed the new movies, the new technology. Enjoyed beautiful food and beautiful women and travel and beaches, but in a sane way. I wish I had.

SL: Is that regret I hear?

JB: Hell, yes! I really missed out. And I am sorry about it, and I am kind of mad and kind of sad, actually. There is no way to get it back. You all have a choice, though.

Stay safe, stay sane, and above all, love life. You will not get a second chance . . . not for a while anyway. So please, make it a very good one. I'll be watching. *[laughs]*

Sending you my best. I wish you all lives filled with fun, love, wonderful experiences, and happiness. Never let go of your curiosity. And above all, remember that life is good. I said so!

Signing off from the great beyond. JB.

SL: Thank you, John.

JB: Sayonara!

Reflections

John finished our interview with "Sayonara," which I thought was very strange! That is generally a sign that I should probe deeper into something, so I looked this up and learned that "Sayonara, sucker!" is a well-known catchphrase of his from the movie *1941.*

I loved reliving those Saturday nights I spent as a teenager, watching John Belushi's antics on TV. My next interview also led me down memory lane to one of my all-time favorite movies, *Dirty Dancing,* and to its incredibly handsome leading man, Patrick Swayze.

CHAPTER 20

PATRICK SWAYZE

When Patrick Swayze appeared to me, I was happy to see that he looked gorgeous and healthy again, much as he did at the height of his career. He had a big grin and beautiful blue eyes, and his energy felt happy, gentle, and peaceful. He appeared wearing blue jeans, a burgundy shirt, and a tan cowboy hat, and he showed me an image of him standing next to a red horse with a light reddish-blond mane and tail.

Patrick Wayne Swayze was born on August 18, 1952, in Houston, Texas. He was an actor, dancer, singer, and songwriter. He starred in many successful films, including *The Outsiders,* the much-beloved *Dirty Dancing,* and *Ghost;* appeared in several TV series; and starred in the original Broadway production of *Grease.* He was an avid horseback rider and pilot. He married his childhood sweetheart, Lisa Niemi, in 1975.

After a nearly two-year battle with pancreatic cancer, he died on September 14, 2009, in Los Angeles at the age of age 57. He said of his death, "The cancer got me, but not permanently."

I remember reading about his fight with cancer while he was still here, and I felt so sad when he passed. It was great to see him doing well again.

The Interview

Susan Lander: Hello, Patrick! It's so nice to meet you.

Patrick Swayze: I'm happy to participate. I relish the opportunity to talk again and bring messages to Lisa and everybody else.

SL: In the movie *Ghost* you played the role of an investment banker who was killed and became a ghost. How has the movie become relevant to you now?

[Rather than a direct response from him, I hear his line from Ghost *about how the love in your heart goes with you to the Other Side.]*

SL: In many of your TV and movie roles, you portrayed bad boys or tough guys. How close were those personas to who you really were?

PS: I am a peaceful fighter, I guess. I know what I want, and I go after it. But you can still be a nice person while you do that and not run over other people. I am one of those—can't we all get along? I think we can if we try.

SL: Did you ever consider giving up the fight against pancreatic cancer?

PS: Oh God, no! I did everything I could to stay here as long as possible. I still believed I would somehow be victorious over it. Maybe some people thought that was delusional, but I didn't. Hope was everything to me.

SL: What advice do you have for people facing similar, life-threatening illnesses?

PS: Fight, fight, fight! Don't give up. There is always hope. It is worth it if you can stay here. Every moment is precious and another opportunity to live, to do something good, to do something you love.

SL: Do you have any regrets? Would you have done anything differently?

PS: None, except leaving too early and having to leave my soul mate, Lisa. Look at my life! It was charmed. I was so happy. I was so lucky. I came here and accomplished what I wanted to accomplish. I had the best companion and soul mate, and she could be with me just about every day. Seriously, what more could I have wanted? I had everything.

SL: How is that for you, for Lisa to be here on Earth when you aren't?

PS: Some people think that it's all angels and harps up here. The truth is that it *is* idyllic, like the best dream ever. No pain, no illness, no suffering. Imagine your perfect world. Beautiful. Gorgeous.

The only problem is that my perfect world is not perfect without Lisa. Until we are together again, I will wait. I spend time with her every day, trying to catch her attention. I want her to be happy and love life on Earth as much as she can. I'll still be with her, until she doesn't want me to be. But, *ouch,* being without her physical body, her physical self, hurts. I just have to deal, though.

Don't get me wrong; I am okay. I will wait for her peacefully until the end of time, if need be. But I don't think I'll have to. Eventually we will be reunited when the time is right, when she is old and gray. But I won't mind. *[smiles]* We don't stay old up here anyway. We can look any way we want, be any way we want. It is one of the good things.

SL: You sent me that line in *Ghost* about how the love in your heart goes with you to the Other Side. So it seems that this is true for you.

PS: *[smiles]* Oh yes, for sure. All the other stuff gets pushed to the side, and what's left is the pure love. We lose all the extra baggage and just carry what's essential. What is pure. What is real. The rest just falls away very quickly—pain, money issues, and the other day-to-day problems that don't seem so little on Earth.

I can imagine people saying, "Him? Money issues?" But the truth is, we all go through the human journey on Earth, and it's sometimes a rocky road for each and every one of us. I am no exception.

I went through a great deal of pain, fear, and loss at the end. It was hard. I sensed my life slipping away and couldn't do anything to stop it. God knows I tried. At a certain point, the body mutinies. So I had to go.

SL: Now that you're on the Other Side, do you have any lingering effects from the illness?

PS: No physical pain, if that's what you mean. We don't have Earth bodies over here, so we don't have pain and illness the way you do. But I'm a little sad, like I said, because I am separated from my soul mate, friends, family, and animal family on Earth. I wish I was still there even if I didn't have optimal health. I didn't have that choice, so it is what it is. I had a very good run. I was lucky; I was blessed—so, like I said, I have no regrets.

SL: What was your favorite movie?

PS: *The Matrix.*

Just kidding—I loved *Dirty Dancing*. That was the transitional movie for me. It was like a big family—Jennifer Grey, especially. True, it wasn't always easy, but I think people love the movie so much because they can sense the love within it and the connection we had to each other. You can't fake that, even if you're the best actor in the world! There's something great to be said for authenticity.

SL: In *Dirty Dancing* you played the role of a seductive but sensitive dance instructor. Is there some advice you can give to aspiring actors and dancers?

PS: Love your craft and be true to yourself. Don't fight it. Don't suppress it. Your very happiness depends on it. I want you to know that you can succeed—just don't give up. Spend some time thinking about and working toward your actual dreams. Think, *What do I want to do?* not just, *I'll do whatever's available.*

Now, I do get the economic realities of Earth. I know that sometimes you have to take jobs just to put food on the table. Still, take the time to get to know yourself, what you like and what you want to do. When you set your sights on something, it has a way of coming into existence and manifesting in your life. I think where people go wrong is that they get beaten down by everyday life, by rejection, and by the illusion of scarcity, so they give up on their dreams. Please don't do that! You really can have it all.

Success is waiting for you. Don't you realize that you are an unlimited being? I can promise you that. And not everything is what it seems on the surface. Look deeper inside. Take the time to really learn about your strengths, your likes and dislikes, and honor them. Then go for it! Believe in yourself and that you can have what you want. Don't let this business get you down. Find what makes you unique and special, and sell it.

SL: You feel like such a happy, peaceful person.

PS: I try. On a good day. *[laughs]*

SL: What is the secret to your happiness?

PS: Wow, I didn't see that one coming! I think it's that I appreciate what I have. I always did. I guess I am a glass-half-full kind of person. You can't go wrong with that sort of attitude, more positive than negative; that way, everything looks good!

SL: Which talent was most important to you—acting or dancing?

PS: Good one! I'll have to think about it . . .
Probably dancing. It was my first real love, like Lisa.

SL: What was your relationship with dance?

PS: It connected me with my soul. It was like a direct line to my heart and my soul.

SL: It seems like you had an amazingly happy marriage. What do you think was the key?

PS: I had someone who understood me and let me be me. And we had mutual respect. I don't think we ever took each other for granted, and we never stopped appreciating each other. We just made room for each other so we could comfortably live out our lives together. It was instinctual and easy with her. I think we understood how special it was. I miss that. I miss her.

SL: What was your favorite achievement—what would you like to be known for?

PS: For making people happy. For giving them an escape from their daily lives if they wanted that. For leaving the world a little better—I hope—than when I came here. I made my little permanent mark on the world.
I loved that I got to meet so many wonderful, talented people in the bargain. My life was such a win-win. So much about it was good; so much worked. I only wish I could have danced on the earth a lot longer. I urge all of you to see the example of what I went through, and just don't waste any of your time here. Fill up every minute with something good. With love, if you can. I am proud to say that

I always tried to do that. So even though I had to leave early, I can look back and say that my life was good, and I did good. I can rest easy and be peaceful. I wish that for all of you.

SL: Do you have any other messages?

PS: Thank you for listening. This has been fun. Just because I'm over here doesn't mean I've turned into Yoda, but I like to believe I have some useful advice to offer. Hindsight is 20/20, and it's all a bit clearer now.

I do want to reiterate my good-byes to everyone, and remind them that I meant every word. I also want to send giant, humongous hugs and kisses to my loves—to Lisa, to my family and friends. I still visit you (yes, that's me), and I try to communicate with you. Never doubt for a minute that I am still here and still a part of your lives. I see your milestones and your celebrations.

I love you, love you, love you with all my heart. I feel great, and I am blissfully happy. Except, Lisa, I miss you so much it hurts. Try to feel my love; it is even bigger and greater than it was, if that's even possible. When you talk to me, I hear you. When you think I'm holding your hand, holding you, I am. Please forgive me for this public message, but I really wanted to get this message to you so you know that I'm really, for sure, totally, absolutely here!

Thank you.

[He bows to me with his hand over his heart.]

SL: You are so welcome.

[Eighteen months later, as I was editing this book, Patrick appeared to me and wouldn't leave until I agreed to add a new message for Lisa. Of course I agreed.]

SL: Patrick, you have a message for Lisa?

PS: Yes, it is really important. Lisa, I know that you have been dating. I'm so happy for you. You must keep on living—that's the most important thing. I want you to be happy, and I don't want you to be alone.

The future will take care of itself. Do not give my feelings a second thought. My feelings are of wholehearted soul love for you. That does not include possessiveness. I wish I could still be with you on Earth, but I can't. Occupying the position of second best will have to do. I can live with that if I know you're happy.

Thank you.

SL: You're welcome. That's it?

PS: Yes. Much love to everyone.

Reflections

I loved connecting with Patrick Swayze and his beautiful energy. Even though talking about the cancer and leaving his wife made him feel sad (and I felt it right along with him), during the rest of the interview I felt as if I were floating in a sea of love and tranquility.

After this interview, I did some research to explore a few of the details that came up. In reference to Patrick's final message to Lisa, I located an article reporting that Lisa had married jeweler Albert DePrisco in May 2014. I wish them all the best.

When Patrick first appeared to me, I saw an image of him standing next to a horse. In researching his connection to horses, I learned that he was passionate about Arabian horses and was very connected to his chestnut stallion, Tammen. There are numerous pictures of Patrick riding him, and he exactly matches the horse I saw at the beginning of the interview. (Also, after the interview, I watched *Ghost* on TV, and I was surprised to see Patrick wearing a burgundy shirt in the movie, just like the one he was wearing when he first appeared to me!)

If you would like to learn more about Patrick Swayze, he and Lisa cowrote his autobiography, *The Time of My Life*, which was published posthumously in 2009.

My next visitor also died of pancreatic cancer, but not until he moved technology light-years ahead and changed the way we communicate forever: Steve Jobs.

―――――――――――――――

CHAPTER 21

STEVE JOBS

I began wondering whether Steve Jobs would talk with me shortly after he passed, but I had not seen or heard from him. Finally I saw him on July 8, 2012, nine months after he passed. He had a big smile and a scruffy silver beard. He was wearing his signature black turtleneck and wire-rimmed glasses. Then I heard the word *innovation.*

Steven Paul Jobs was born on February 24, 1955, in San Francisco, California. He was adopted and grew up in Cupertino, located in the area now known as Silicon Valley. He was a pioneer and visionary in the field of personal computers and electronics. With Stephen Wozniak, he co-founded Apple Computer in 1977, which quickly became a Fortune 500 company. In 1985 he was ousted by the board of directors at Apple, and he immediately started another computer firm, NeXT Inc., designing workstation computers for the educational sector.

In 1986 Steve acquired a controlling interest in Pixar and built it into a major animation studio. Under his leadership, Pixar produced *Toy Story* in 1995, the first full-length computer-animated film—the company's public stock offering the next year made Steve a billion-aire. (He sold Pixar to the Walt Disney Company in 2006.)

Apple began struggling financially, and brought Steve back as a consultant in 1996. By the next year, he was leading Apple once again, and saved the nearly bankrupt company with a series of innovative personal computers. The iMac desktop debuted in 1998, followed by the iBook laptop. Apple introduced iTunes and the iPod to the world in 2001, and the iPhone in 2007.

Steve Jobs died of pancreatic cancer on October 5, 2011, in Palo Alto, California, at the age of 56.

Even though I had asked for him over and over, when he arrived I suddenly felt shy and intimidated! After all, this was a man who had changed the world, as well as people's lives (including mine), for the better in a very personal way.

The Interview

Steve Jobs: *[noticing my nervousness]* Oh, no need to feel that way. I'm just an orphan who made good. I had plenty of ideas that didn't take flight. The secret of my success was that I acted on my ideas. You just have to be willing to try, and to do the hard work.

[He pulls my attention to a postcard I have on my refrigerator, featuring the line: "What would you try to do if you knew you could not fail?"]

As long as you try, you have not failed. What counts is the effort. So don't hold back, and make the most of your opportunities to try new things.

Susan Lander: Why do you think Apple has been so incredibly successful?

SJ: In some ways, our devices are like the best lovers. They give you just what you need and are there for you without question.

That's my secret, the secret to the success of Apple computers. They are intuitive; they are streamlined to work with you. They feel like you. We went for the experience.

SL: How did you know to do that?

SJ: The heart. The intuition. No project or item is going to be a bestseller unless the consumer makes a heart connection with it. Heart first, then head. That is another secret of my success. If you can touch someone's heart, then you can help them feel happy, fulfilled, and taken care of. I was glad that I could be a part of that.

You do also need a business sense to become very successful—or at least good advisors!

SL: Where did your ideas come from?

SJ: I just thought, *What would I want to do? What would I want to have?* I took the time to ask myself the questions, and I asked other people, too. Then I envisioned a prototype and got the best team together to make it happen.

I always employed dreamers like myself. Futuristic people who weren't afraid to innovate. You have nothing to lose by dreaming big. If the first prototype failed (and believe me, many of them did), we just picked ourselves up and tried again. Tweaked things. We just had the vision out in front of us and made things happen. We kept going until we reached our vision, our Mecca, our Holy Grail.

SL: What made you develop the iPhone?

SJ: I just wanted a computer that I could carry with me. It was the next logical step in the development of our products. It didn't make sense to only work on making computers better . . . of course, we wanted to keep making them better! But we also wanted to keep making them smaller, more useful, more portable. And, eventually, more indispensable.

It's not that we wanted to create an artificial need. It was just an idea whose time had come. Society was ready for it, and it could make everything better. It was a very symbiotic relationship. Like the chicken or the egg . . . which came first, the need or the idea?

SL: I noticed that you usually say "we" and "ours" as opposed to "me." Why is that?

SJ: I was acutely aware that my success was a team effort. No man is an island, least of all in technology. It requires many dedicated people to bring a product to market, to advertise it, to get it out there, to sell it. I loved my team. I could not have been a success without them. My success is shared with them. I hope they know how much I value them. I am still watching over them and keeping an eye on things. I feel that I gave birth to this company. I am so proud of it and what I accomplished while I was on Earth. I am one proud father!

SL: Do you know about the recent concerns about working conditions at a Foxconn Technology Group factory in China that makes iPhones and iPads?

SJ: Yes, of course I do. It is so hard, such a challenge, to bring quality goods at affordable prices to the consumer. It is challenging to properly oversee working conditions overseas. Of course, we tried. We need to try harder. It makes me so sad. We are in the business of making people happy, not taking advantage of or traumatizing them. But it is very complicated socioeconomically.

I hope that those I left in charge will take these complaints very, very seriously, and that they will take steps to remedy them. I am not there anymore. It is their job now to man (and woman) the company. I have faith in them to do the right thing for all who are involved in this issue. The workers, the company, everybody. This is their path now. They came here to be innovators; that's why they ended up working for me. They need to come up with solutions so we don't all end up looking like schmucks. We have our reputations to consider!

Seriously, though, it matters to me what happens with this company. It is my baby, my legacy. It is important to me that it do business in a reputable way. I am no longer at the helm, but I am still here, and I see what happens. I hold them accountable for what happens in my name.

This is not to blame anybody. But I was as human as anyone else, so I understand the tendency to put off dealing with unpleasant things until it becomes necessary. Enough said. I love them. I am not upset. I mean that. This is all part of the learning and growing that we must do on Earth, and that we continue to do on the Other Side. It's just that we have so many more chances to be stellar while on Earth. *[smiles]* And to make positive, uplifting, and innovative choices while we're there. To make great changes for humanity. We can at least strive to leave Earth better than we found it.

SL: Do you think that you did that?

SJ: Yes, I do. I experienced a very personal relationship with everything I created. That's the nature of creativity; it is personal. I let it have its freedom and didn't limit it, and it grew and grew and grew.

SL: Do you have any regrets?

SJ: I tried to fight my illness, but I lost. I would have liked more time to invent, develop, create, and give back to all of you for everything you've given me.

Still, I am so happy with the way my life turned out. It was amazing. It was huge. I am so grateful for it. I loved my life, my wife and kids, my extended family. I was a lucky man. I am grateful to my birth parents for giving me a fighting chance at life. I am grateful to my parents who adopted and raised me, and who encouraged me to be me. Thank you, thank you, thank you.

It was a wild ride. Too short, but so wild and wonderful. Looking back, I almost feel like I held my breath all the way through, just waiting with excitement about what unknown thing—or miracle— was going to happen next. What a great way to go through life!

Please believe in yourself. This is your time—take it. Never live for other people and their expectations . . . for that can never make you happy. You are your most important person, your VIP. I give you a gold star for being you.

Please spend some time getting to know yourself, learning what you like, what you don't like, want you want, and what you don't want. Never sell yourself short or disrespect the real you. Set your vision. Set your sights high; don't lower them. Never limit yourself or what you want to accomplish, because if you do that, you are setting your own limits—and trust me, you will live down to them.

Picture the best future you can imagine; set that vision into place. Then go for it! Do not be deterred. In the world you live in, there is unlimited abundance and potential for your success. As they say, if you can dream it, you can be it, and you can have it. You can have everything you want; just don't give up on your dream. Reach for that brass ring every day.

Sending you all my love from heaven. Believe me, it is good here. But if I had my choice, I would still be there with you, dreaming my big, crazy, improbable dreams—then making them happen.

SL: How are you now?

SJ: I want people to know that I am safe. I am good. I am not sick anymore. I have a feeling of peace, and when I look back and think about my lifetime, I feel proud. I have the feeling of a job well done.

And I am getting ready for my next show! You can't hold a good man down for long.

SL: Does that mean you're coming back?

SJ: Soon, but I'm taking a rest first and enjoying some downtime. But I think it will be pretty soon. I have more to do. More inventions, innovations, technology to make. I am not finished yet. You haven't seen the last of me, although I won't look the same the next time. *[smiles]* Maybe I'll come back as a woman. Now that would be interesting to explore, to see if I can get as far.

SL: What was your greatest accomplishment?

SJ: Every new thing that worked the way I wanted it to work gave me a sense of accomplishment.

SL: What was your greatest joy?

SJ: My children. And the rush of energy that comes with making something new.

I have a message for my children, my wife, my sister, and my extended family: Hello, all of you! Here I am, back to say hello. I am so sorry and so sad that I had to leave you. I tried hard to stay—you know I did—and I still can't believe it got me. You know I am such a fighter, and I thought I would win. But at any rate . . .

I love you so much. That hasn't changed, and it never will. I still visit you every day. I try to visit you in your dreams so you can see me and know I'm still with you. Please know that this is real. You are not making it up. I'm still a part of your life, just from afar. And I'm much lighter now. *[smiles]* But I'm still me, and I still love you. Always remember that.

SL: What was your greatest disappointment?

SJ: Leaving too early.

SL: How would you like to be remembered?

SJ: As an innovator who left the world a better place than it was when he got here. Someone who changed the way the world communicates and made the extraordinary commonplace. A game changer.

SL: What ideas were you working on or thinking about when you left?

SJ: A special sleeve.

[He shows me an image of something that looks like a sleeve with buttons on it. It has something to do with charging.]

SL: I get the feeling that you really enjoyed this conversation. Have you?

SJ: Immensely! I'm participating in a new kind of communication across the dimensions. There's nothing better than that. Maybe I can build a computer or device to help it along. *[smiles]* Just kidding! On the other hand, maybe not. Maybe there's a way . . . I'll have to think about it.

SL: *[sensing empty airspace]* Are we done?

SJ: We're done. For now.

Reflections

I was in awe when Steve left. Even as a spirit, he was full of fascinating, innovative thoughts. His words came through very quickly and coherently, with warm feelings that I could only describe as "heart." I have never met anyone, human or spirit, who is like him. He is completely solid and secure in who he is, and still as brilliant, curious, and creative as he was while he was on Earth.

My next guest was another innovative thinker, the writer Kurt Vonnegut. Ironically, his many books and plays often discussed the possible dehumanizing effects of technology on our future.

CHAPTER 22

KURT VONNEGUT

This interview is unusual in that it happened as a three-way conversation between Kurt Vonnegut, my friend Fran, and me. Fran is very familiar with his work, having adapted his book *Mother Night* into a play.

When this interview occurred, Fran and I were having dinner at one of the many outdoor cafés on the Upper West Side of Manhattan. It was a clear and perfect summer evening, and just as I mentioned to Fran that I'd like to interview Kurt, he immediately popped in. He was casually dressed in khaki pants and a comfortable-looking yellow-gold shirt. He had a mustache, and his salt-and-pepper hair was thick and just a little bit shaggy. He just felt very comfortable to be around. I immediately turned on my phone's recorder and began asking him questions. Kurt gave me his responses, which I repeated out loud to Fran.

Kurt Vonnegut, Jr., was born on November 11, 1922, in Indianapolis, Indiana. He wrote award-winning novels, essays, short stories, and plays, whose appeal continues to endure across generations, with a mix of satire, humor, and science fiction. He is considered one of the great American writers of the 20th century. His most famous works include: *The Sirens of Titan, Cat's Cradle, Slaughterhouse-Five,* and *Breakfast of Champions.* (*Breakfast of Champions* is known for his signature sketch, which looks kind of like an asterisk but is meant to represent an asshole. Seriously.)

Kurt served in the Army in World War II and was captured by the Germans. His experiences as a prisoner of war greatly affected him and served as the basis for *Slaughterhouse-Five.* He also suffered from depression and tried to commit suicide in 1984. Fortunately, none of this dampened his incredible sense of humor or his ability to embrace the absurd in everyday life.

He died in New York City on April 11, 2007, at the age of 84, of a brain injury sustained after falling on the steps of his brownstone. He said his cause of death was "Internal injuries. I fell. Kerplunk."

The Interview

Susan Lander: Kurt, what is the main message you want to give to those reading this book?

Kurt Vonnegut: My main message is to writers.

SL: Nice. Thank you! Tell me your writing process.

KV: Rewrites, rewrites, rewrites!

Fran: Could you ask him, did he work straight ahead, or did he move back and forth between new stuff and old stuff?

KV: New stuff . . . old stuff . . . new stuff . . . old stuff.

SL: When did you like to write?

[to Fran] He's showing me a cup of coffee. He liked to write in the morning, with his morning coffee.

How did you get your subject matter?

KV: It was based on my personal history and things I wanted to write about. And "what-ifs." "What if?" is a great question. "What-ifs" are the fertile soil of the imagination.

SL: What is your favorite food?

KV: Brownies. The breakfast of champions.

F: That's a pun. *Breakfast of Champions* is the title of one of his books. I thought you knew that.

SL: No, I didn't know that.

F: That's why I'm here. I'm your Vonnegut interpreter!

[to Kurt] Are you pleased with the movie adaptations of your books? Like *Slaughterhouse-Five, Breakfast of Champions,* and *Mother Night*?

KV: Imitation is the sincerest form of flattery. While it doesn't matter now how much I loved them or didn't love them, I thought the movies were all good. *Slaughterhouse-Five* was my favorite.

My books were on the pulse of the moment, and I'm happy that people felt moved and motivated to make them into movies. It means my books touched something. The fact that people were willing to watch them, and are still willing to watch them and read my books, feels very important to me.

F: After I did *Mother Night,* I met with Kurt's agent, and he asked whether there was anything else I wanted to adapt. I said *Player Piano,* one of the first books that Kurt wrote. The story itself is a little dated, but its philosophy is not. It has to do with technology. In the story, society becomes so mechanized that it takes away a lot of jobs, and there is an uprising of the masses. The rebels lose, and one of the main characters asks, "So why did we do this?" The answer was, "For the record." It's a historical note that somebody took a stand. He keeps referring to an Indian battle . . .

SL: He's talking about the Battle of the Little Bighorn in Montana Territory in 1876. Chief Sitting Bull led the Sioux Nation and defeated federal troops led by Lieutenant Colonel George Custer. They took a stand in order to protect their freedom and their sacred land, which was being taken over by gold miners.

F: They did it for the record. Today there's so much emphasis on winning. Sometimes it's enough to take a stand, and that's why I always wanted to turn *Player Piano* into a play.

SL: It's very relevant! It's exactly what we're looking at today, machines taking over people's jobs.

[to Kurt] How relevant do you feel your books are today?

KV: I do feel that my books have special relevance because we need to not lose the value of human life and livelihood in the name of expediency, corporate welfare, and cheap profits. It's about the choices that we make as a society. We need to make choices about how we spend our money and the things we value. Humans should never be subsumed by machines. We need to actually choose, as opposed to letting things slide by.

SL: What message do you have for humanity?

KV: *[laughs]* I just like to share my stories, and if people learn something from them, great! I feel like I have something to share, but "the big lessons for humanity" concept seems kind of grandiose for me. Message for humanity . . . message for humanity . . . message for humanity . . . value the right things! Were you hoping for something more eloquent?

F: Do you have any messages for writers?

KV: Write and write and write. Do it because you can. Do it because you love to. Always be satisfied with what you write, but never be too satisfied. Stay hungry. But appreciate what you do, and appreciate that you're doing it.

Words are very powerful. As soon as we had words, we wrote on whatever we could find—papyrus, leaves, cave walls! It's the way we have connected and communicated since the dawn of time.

Now it's so much easier. Even though in some ways computers and mass markets are impersonal, it allows us to share our individual messages with so many more people. Everyone is an original thinker at heart. I think writers fall prey to feeling like their words are not good enough. But that's not true. Every word that you write from your heart is important, and worth something, because it's a reflection of who you are.

If I could share some wise words with writers, it's to never sell yourself short. Always value what you write. Always think it's good enough. Just do it, that's the important thing. That's the danger for writers. They get depressed, they get overwhelmed, or they feel like they can't produce.

You don't need to produce salable books or magazine articles or journals or whatever is your preferred media. You don't need to base your success on what you sell, because sales are based on other people's opinions, and that doesn't matter when you're a writer. It matters to what you sell, but it doesn't matter to who you are. And it should not, above all, matter to your identity as a writer.

Cherish that you write. Try to love your words. And never compare yourself to anybody else. If you compare your writing to somebody else's, or if you try to mimic another's writing, you're not being an original thinker. You'll also lose the heart and the soul of what you create, and the cost to your own work is going to be considerable.

Even though Fran adapted *Mother Night,* she put her own spin on it. If you're working on an adaptation, adding your own input is important.

Originality is everything. It's your worth and your value as a writer and as a person. The beauty of that is that you will get your best results by being yourself. And if somebody doesn't like it, fuck 'em!

I know it's hard for writers who want to sell to think this way—you have to make a living. But if you try to pigeonhole yourself into this genre or that genre, it's very dangerous to the creative process. If I could give one message to writers, it's to please not fall into that trap.

I feel like the secret of my success was my originality, with my truth at center stage. Even if it's fiction, build around the truth and put that at the center.

Trust your own creative process. If you want to study other people's work, that's fine, to give you ideas. But never be a slave to other people's processes or their ideas. Trust yourself. If you work from your heart and your truth, you will eventually be noticed.

When you come to Earth to be a writer, you're coming here to express yourself through your writing. Remember it that way. Don't come here as your ghostwriter! People don't want to hear other people's perspectives from you; they want to hear yours. Otherwise you're just a copycat, and that gets old. So write as you. Just give yourself the freedom to work your way, and to talk about what you want to talk about.

There are always certain words in writers' hearts. I encourage you to think about what that is: What is that piece of writing that wants to be born? If you tried it before and it didn't quite work, give it a rebirth. Your writing can be born again and again and again. Even if it's the same subject matter, you can do so much with it. It's all very fertile ground.

F: This answers my question. I was wondering whether something I did was okay when I adapted *Mother Night*. I changed what happened to one of the characters. In the book, one of the characters commits suicide, but I was thinking, *What if she woke up the next day instead?*

KV: You should expand; of course you should. That's the point. Keep spinning it out. Have fun! I'm happy that my work inspires you.

F: He answered the question before I asked it. That's so cool!

SL: Spirits do that sometimes. They can hear you thinking it.

KV: What I would not want is for you to be stagnant in your writing. The expansion and the insertion of your originality is what makes it interesting. It is fine with me for you to experiment with my premise. I'm not here, but even if I were, it would be okay with me! I support young writers.

Search your heart for what you want to be writing, and maybe others will inspire you, too. And just keep going. Always stretch as a writer and a creative being, because we have limitless potential. Everyone, even those who are not writers, has creative potential. But writers in particular know how to put that down on paper, so go to it.

Like I said, my favorite question is: "What if?" It's how you know where you're going next. It is the writer's best tool and best friend. You'll be fine as long as you keep asking, "What if?"

SL: That's genius. What inspired your work more than anything?

KV: My personal truths. And the truths that I didn't tell anybody, except in my books.

F: I loved his prefaces. He put so much personal stuff in them. Sometimes they're as long as 40 pages, and they're wonderful. Like the preface of *Welcome to the Monkey House,* where he wrote, "In the water, I am beautiful."

KV: Writing was cathartic for me. It saved my life. It allowed me to process everything I'd been through—all the hard things, all the wonderful things. It was nice for me to be able to look back at my body of work and see my own history.

I feel satisfied with what I accomplished during my lifetime.

SL: Thank you, Kurt, for answering my question before I asked it! I always ask my interviewees that question.

KV: We know!

SL: But did you accomplish what you came to Earth to accomplish?

KV: Oh yes, most definitely! I would have written for another 100 years if I could have, but I had a good long run.

F: Something happened to me that was such a Vonnegut moment, and I always wanted to tell him. I even drafted a letter once. When you read someone's stuff so much, you feel like you know them, but you don't. So I didn't send it then, but I want to share it now.

I went to college in New York. When I graduated in 1972, it was two years after the Kent State shootings, and it was a very popular choice for seniors to not go to graduation. So the school went out of their way to get us there; there was no rehearsal, and we could sit with whomever we wanted, so I was there with a group of friends. My parents had driven up from Long Island. After they read our names, they said "I now confer upon you the degree of Bachelor of Arts with all the rights and privileges inherent in it."

Now, the Vietnam War was still on, four unarmed college students had been shot by the Ohio National Guard during a protest at Kent State, and we were English majors. It was the first time we'd heard about our "rights and privileges," and the absurdity of the statement hit us. So we cracked up laughing. Our parents were horrified. They were paying all this tuition, and their kids are laughing. It just felt like one of those absurdist Vonnegut moments to me, and I always felt like he would understand. So we've got a college education . . . now what the hell are we going to do with it? And so you laugh.

I always wanted to share that with you, Kurt. So thank you.

KV: You're welcome, and thank you for sharing it.

SL: So, Kurt, what is the funniest thing about life?

KV: Everything.

SL: *[to Fran]* He's showing me random images of things he thinks can be funny, like pants and traffic lights.

F: Restaurants that don't take charge cards.

SL: Exactly.

KV: That is Fran's point; there is so much about life that's funny. Even if something is bad, if you can laugh, it makes it better. Sometimes all you can do is laugh because life is so absurd—even if it's absurdly bad.

F: Like the "rights and privileges" of an English major?

KV: Exactly. That's a fantastic story, because it illustrates my point. Education is a great thing, but in the context of war it's laughable! Although that doesn't mean it's not worthy. The funniest thing about life is how, given a different context, so much is absurd.

That's why there is limitless fodder for things that can be funny. Most people are no comedians, but most people can be funny. Most people can see the humor in things, and most people can laugh, even when life is really challenging.

SL: He's making me feel really emotional! All of a sudden I feel like I want to cry. The importance of laughter is a really profound thing for him.

F: But then people think that if you're laughing, you aren't taking something seriously enough.

KV: No, if you lose the humor in life, you lose something precious. Our sense of humor, our ability to see the lighter side of life, and our ability to see things as funny is our birthright. And laughter is good for you! The saddest thing is people who cannot see things as funny. Because then they're just depressed.

SL: That's so true!

F: I had a dream that I was at a funeral the week before Kurt died, and I was wondering whether it was Kurt's funeral.

KV: I wouldn't know; it was Fran's dream! But when I got back to the Other Side, people were celebrating . . . they were either celebrating or they were trying to kick my butt back out! I said, "Are you happy to see me?" They said no . . .

SL: He's just joking.

KV: Go back, do not pass "go," and do not collect 200 dollars!

F: Did Kurt know he was going to pass? Because he had a head injury; he fell.

KV: I had a sense that time was short. I was up there in years. But it wasn't bad. And then when I came back to the Other Side, people really were celebrating. I had a big party. With canapés.

F: Kurt, that's so 1950s. My mom used to make canapés—they're like little toasts with stuff on them. But they're elegant.

SL: Fran, he might be giving you a message from your mom, like a little postcard from the Other Side to say hello. Spirits find ways to get messages to us, even if she had to ask Kurt to deliver the message!

F: Who does Kurt hang with on the Other Side?

SL: Aw, he's showing me Snoopy from the *Peanuts* comic strip! So he's referencing Charles Schulz, the artist who drew him.

[to Kurt] Who else are you spending time with?

KV: I have other literary friends. Authors like F. Scott Fitzgerald. Some war friends.

F: Has Kurt bumped into William Shakespeare? What does he think of Shakespeare as a person, as a writer?

KV: He's brooding.

F: I didn't think anybody brooded on the Other Side. Seriously?

KV: He's a creative genius. He's intense.

F: Did Shakespeare really write all his own plays?

KV: He says so!

F: What about Sophocles, the playwright from ancient Greece? Has he met Sophocles?

KV: He's old.

SL: *[to Fran]* He's making a joke. Nobody is old on the Other Side.

I'm seeing Judy Garland. *[to Kurt]* Are you friends with her?

KV: Yes. It's like on Earth. Some of our friends are more similar to us, and some are very different.

F: Did Kurt enjoy writing plays when he was on Earth?

KV: Yeah, it's a nice place to visit, but I wouldn't want to live there all of the time.

SL: What was your favorite thing here on Earth?

KV: My kids.

F: Didn't one of his children have some type of mental illness?

KV: Yes, he's a special soul. People who come to Earth to experience severe developmental, mental, learning, or physical disabilities are special because they're going to have a hard path in this society. It is an opportunity for them to learn a lot as well as to teach others.

F: Are they "old souls" who have been around a long time?

KV: Old souls, or brave young ones.

F: In one of his more recent books, *Bluebeard,* the main character was a painter living out in the Hamptons. Did he base this character on the artist Jackson Pollock?

KV: It was a conglomeration. A little bit of this, a little bit of that.

F: What was his favorite place? Did he like the beach?

KV: I loved the beach. I was a New Yorker; of course I used to go to the beach. I used to spend summers there.

SL: *[to Fran]* I'm seeing an image of him when he was really young. I feel like it was the Hamptons on Long Island. Now he's showing me a bicycle. Maybe that was something he liked to do?

F: People used to bike out in the Hamptons, too.

SL: Aah, we've been talking an hour. This is going to be a hellish interview to transcribe. What else?

KV: I'm happy. I'm at peace. My peace is not boring. I'm not up here playing a harp.

SL: I'm seeing him playing an electric guitar!

KV: Heaven is not boring.

F: It shouldn't be. It wouldn't be heaven if it were boring.

SL: Are you writing?

KV: It's more like creating. Creating is high art here, and it's very valued. It should be valued as much on Earth, but it's only valued on Earth if you make a lot of money.

SL: That's so true! And it's so not fair.

KV: It's a value judgment placed upon the money and not the work. You've got to be really careful about placing the value of your writing on your commercial success. This is where so many writers go wrong. What people think is so random and subjective. Whether something will be published or successful is random. Even our economy is random.

It's like everything else in life; sometimes you're lucky, and sometimes you're not. Sometimes you're in the right place at the right time, and sometimes you're not. But I will say this, the better you feel about your work and the more you do of it, the more you're likely to sell. More people will notice you. That part of it is just a numbers game.

Love your work, even if it's bad. Love it because it's yours.

[Kurt brings my attention back to the outdoor café where Fran and I are seated.]

KV: This is so nice. I really miss New York City. Especially in the spring and the summer, when the weather is really beautiful like this. The city is so vibrant, and it comes alive at night . . . it has that special energy, and everybody gets excited and happy.

F: Kurt, what's your favorite food?

SL: He's showing me the scene in Disney's *Lady and the Tramp* with the two dogs pulling the spaghetti. So it's spaghetti and meatballs.

KV: And a nice chianti.

F: And fava beans? *[That's a reference to a famous line from the movie* Silence of the Lambs.*]*

SL: Exactly! He's also showing me chocolate pudding and a Danish pastry.

KV: And don't forget women! Add them to the list, please.

SL: Done.

KV: Is there anything else you would like to know?

SL: Do you have any more advice for writers?

KV: As I said, my advice for writers is to always be yourself. Never feel ashamed to show who you are. Never be ashamed to show your vulnerability. Be proud of your art and your creativity, no matter what form it takes.
Anything innovative can raise anxiety in writers because it's unknown. It's like the unease we have when we feel that we're different. There is pressure to toe the line, pressure to adhere to a formula or a category.

F: Definitely for categories, like mysteries or romance. I read a few books by one author where the big sex scene between the male and female leads is always around page 220! So of course I would go to those pages. But it was too formulaic for me, and I stopped reading her.

KV: It's funny; people love to read about sex.

F: Those who can't do, can't write!

KV: It's hard to write good sex, but people still like to read about sex even if it's not written well.

F: The first sex scene I ever wrote, what was funny about it was that when you do it, it's spontaneous. But when you write it, it's like "He put his hand there, so I put my hand here," and I'm mimicking all these gestures in my room. When I looked up, I could see the reflections of all my movements in the monitor, and I blushed and laughed at the same time, because it was just so weird.

KV: We're back to the absurd. You've got to laugh at it, because it's funny!

F: I don't remember reading a real sex scene in Kurt's books. Did he write any sex scenes?

KV: Not well.

F: I had a writing teacher give me the best advice. Don't put anything in that you would be embarrassed to do, or it will add a level of awkwardness to your writing and the audience won't buy it. It has to be something you're comfortable with. Does Kurt agree with that?

KV: Yes. Self-consciousness is a problem in sex scenes when you're writing them. The important thing about sex scenes and writing sex is that they have heart. People want to know that there's a connection between the people having sex. That's the key.

Where angels fear to tread . . . is into writing sex scenes!

People are funny; they love sex so much that even bad sex is good sex, for most of them.

F: Sometimes I think bad sex is more honest. In movies when the first sex scenes aren't comfortable, it comes off as more real to me sometimes.

KV: Yes. The most pivotal, important thing about sex scenes is the honesty. You're absolutely right!

F: Like in the movie *The Big Easy.*

SL: Oh my God. That has one of the best sex scenes I've ever seen, and most of their clothes stay on! It's such an honest-feeling scene. And self-conscious . . . it's amazing. So you're right—even bad sex is good sex if it's honest.

KV: Good night, ladies. I bid you adieu. It was an absolute pleasure.

[He sends me a wave of warm feelings.]

SL: Thank you so much, Kurt.

F: Thank you, Kurt.

KV: You're welcome! Thank you for interviewing me, and I look forward to seeing my words in your book.

SL: He's showing me fireworks.

F: Maybe it's a nice farewell.

SL: It's the finale!

[It took me a week to transcribe this interview. During this time I also read Kurt's book A Man Without a Country: A Memoir of Life in George W. Bush's America. *I was captivated by a particular quote, so I decided to follow up with him and ask him about it.]*

SL: Kurt, I loved this interview. Thank you again. I have two follow-up questions.

KV: Shoot.

SL: In your book *A Man Without a Country,* you said: "The truth is, we know so little about life, we don't really know what the good news is and what the bad news is. And if I die—God forbid—I would like to go to heaven to ask somebody in charge up there, 'Hey, what was the good news and what was the bad news?'"

So what was the good news and what was the bad news about life?

KV: The bad news is, if you don't do it just right, you have to do it all over again.

Just kidding. The great tribunal up here isn't that unforgiving. We are really masters of our own destiny. And that is both the good news and the bad news. You do things right, you get the credit. You screw up, you get the credit for that, too. You are at the beginning. You are at the end. What do you want your middle to look like?

SL: Are you planning to come back here? If so, what would you be?

KV: A frog. Just kidding. I wouldn't be anything so green.

Reflections

Kurt has given me some final words to add to these Reflections. He wishes to say that he enjoyed coming back once again to share his thoughts with a willing audience. He thinks he's even smarter than he used to be, but as you can see from that statement alone, he's still an "asshole"—or at least a smart-aleck.

Personally, however, I didn't think he was either of those. I thought he was brilliant, deeply insightful, witty, and warm. This was one of my very favorite interviews. If you haven't read any of his books, I would highly recommend doing so now.

Following the interview, I did some Internet research and found an interesting synchronicity. Kurt's answer for his favorite food was: "Brownies. The breakfast of champions." Fran noted that it was a pun, because *Breakfast of Champions* is the title of one of his books. However, I discovered that the word *brownies* was also significant. In his book *Cat's Cradle,* Chapter 23 is titled "The Last Batch of Brownies." However, the "brownie" wasn't actually food; it was a piece of technology. It was the last gift this character created for humankind before he died.

I thought this seemed like an appropriate tie-in, given the nature of this book. These interviews are final gifts of wisdom from these 22 generous and openhearted spirits.

AFTERWORD

Now it's my turn to look back at my journey since this book began. It has been amazing, challenging, surprising, and intense. I think it's fair to say that it has changed me for the better. The wisdom that these spirits shared with me benefitted me personally, and it is my hope that it will help you, the reader, to build a happier, more peaceful, more prosperous life.

The most important lesson I've learned is this: there's no need to be afraid of life, so jump in and take action on your dreams. What's the worst thing that could happen? If you're smart and even a little bit introspective, you'll learn something, and you'll always come out ahead.

Working on this book reinforced what I already knew: there is limitless wisdom out there just waiting to be received. What form our teachers take varies from person to person, but everyone has them. Life—and even the afterlife—is arranged so we can always teach, and learn from, each other. The key is just to see it and to be open to the lessons.

Be kind to (or at least look benevolently upon) all our soul mates who came along with us for this ride we call life. Even though it may not necessarily seem like it while we're here, they are always our allies.

Most of all, I've had fun doing these interviews, and I hope you've enjoyed reading them.

ACKNOWLEDGMENTS

I am sending my most heartfelt gratitude to all of the souls who participated in this project, both on this side and the other, who contributed to this project in a myriad of ways. Without all of you, this would never have happened. You have all enriched my life in ways I never could have imagined, and I can only hope that I have done right by all of you. I love learning from you every day.

On this side, first and foremost, I want to thank my sister, Fern Sandler, and my parents, Madeline and Lowell Lander, for their loving support and belief in me and in this project. I also want to give a special shout-out to my mother for her patience in rereading and re-editing this book, and to my niece and nephew, Rachel and Adam, who are used to living spirit-filled lives and always serve as an example to me. I also want to thank Rachel and Adam for contributing insightful questions.

I want to send special gratitude for my teachers and mentors along the way, especially Dr. Christine Page, Rabbi Jill Hammer,

Sonia Choquette, and Lisa Williams, who helped me find my spirit's voice so I could give voice to the spirits of others.

Sending lots of gratitude to my friends who have listened patiently while I read them interview after interview, suggested new interviews, supported me steadfastly, and contributed the occasional excellent question: Steve and Karen, John and Louise, Mary Ellen and Dan, Sydney, Amy, Ginger, Robin, Lisa, Roland, Nancy, Laurie, Michelle, Judy, Kristen, Joel, Mark, Dave, David, the Saxes, Jocelyn and Idalie, Sherri and Carol, Carolyn and Charlie, and Rev. Carol. Thank you to Frances Miksits for her contribution to this book, to Kristine Gasbarre for her fabulous editing, and to Steve Bacher for the subtitle. Finally, thank you to my doctors for making sure that this book got written!

I want to thank everyone at Hay House for giving me the opportunity to publish this book and get it out into the world, especially Reid Tracy, Stacey Smith, Christy Salinas, Shannon Littrell, Alex Freemon, Nicolette Salamanca, and Cheryl Richardson. I also want to thank Michelle Buchanan for her help and guidance.

I want to thank my Romemu family for their love and support, and for always reminding me of the true meaning of service. And, of course, there is always Lia. In this story that is my life, I know that all of you are there, and that means everything.

I also want to thank Julia Cameron and Emma Lively for helping me open the door to reimagining and jump-starting my new life as a writer, and for giving me a new way to allow spirit to come through.

Love and blessings to all of you, and to all of those who read this book.

ABOUT THE AUTHOR

Susan Lander is a lawyer, writer, and psychic medium who spent 20 years in the legal field before transitioning to a career honoring her very special gift: the ability to communicate with spirits. A lifelong clairvoyant and a message medium, Susan is able to see, hear, and feel spirits, and to transmit their emotional messages from the Other Side. Using her unique combination of psychic, analytical, and teaching skills, Susan has led hundreds of seminars on the topics of spiritual and psychic development, leadership, law, and public speaking. She lives in New York City.

To learn more, please visit: www.susanlander.us.

We hope you enjoyed this Hay House book.
If you'd like to receive our online catalog featuring additional information on
Hay House books and products, or if you'd like to find out more about the
Hay Foundation, please contact:

Hay House, Inc., P.O. Box 5100, Carlsbad, CA 92018-5100
(760) 431-7695 or (800) 654-5126
(760) 431-6948 (fax) or (800) 650-5115 (fax)
www.hayhouse.com® • www.hayfoundation.org

Published and distributed in Australia by: Hay House Australia Pty. Ltd.,
18/36 Ralph St., Alexandria NSW 2015
Phone: 612-9669-4299 • *Fax:* 612-9669-4144 • www.hayhouse.com.au

Published and distributed in the United Kingdom by: Hay House UK, Ltd.,
Astley House, 33 Notting Hill Gate, London W11 3JQ
Phone: 44-20-3675-2450 • *Fax:* 44-20-3675-2451 • www.hayhouse.co.uk

Published and distributed in the Republic of South Africa by:
Hay House SA (Pty), Ltd., P.O. Box 990, Witkoppen 2068
Phone/Fax: 27-11-467-8904 • www.hayhouse.co.za

Published in India by: Hay House Publishers India,
Muskaan Complex, Plot No. 3, B-2, Vasant Kunj, New Delhi 110 070
Phone: 91-11-4176-1620 • *Fax:* 91-11-4176-1630 • www.hayhouse.co.in

Distributed in Canada by: Raincoast Books, 2
440 Viking Way, Richmond, B.C. V6V 1N2
Phone: 1-800-663-5714 • *Fax:* 1-800-565-3770 • www.raincoast.com

Take Your Soul on a Vacation

Visit www.HealYourLife.com® to regroup,
recharge, and reconnect with your own magnificence.
Featuring blogs, mind-body-spirit news, and
life-changing wisdom from Louise Hay and friends.

Visit www.HealYourLife.com today!